Paper Cutting Techniques for Scrapbooks & Cards

Crowds of bees are
giddy with clover
Crowds of grasshoppers
dance at our feet
Crowds of larks at their
matins hang over
Thanking the Lord for
a life so sweet

Paper Cutting Techniques for Scrapbooks & Cards

Sharyn Sowell

STERLING/CHAPELLE
An imprint of Sterling Publishing Co., Inc.

New York / London
www.sterlingpublishing.com

Chapelle, Ltd., Inc., P.O. Box 9252, Ogden, UT 84409
(801) 621-2777 • (801) 621-2788 Fax
e-mail: chapelle@chapelleltd.com
Web site: www.chapelleltd.com

This volume is meant to stimulate decorating ideas. If readers are unfamiliar or not proficient in a skill necessary to attempt a project, we urge that they refer to an instructional book specifically addressing the required technique.

Library of Congress Cataloging-in-Publication Data

Sowell, Sharyn.
Paper cutting techniques for scrapbooks & cards / Sharyn Sowell.
p. cm.
"A Sterling/Chapelle Book."
Includes index.
ISBN 1-4027-1921-3
1. Paper work. 2. Scrapbooks. 3. Greeting cards. I. Title.

TT870.S672 2005
736'.98--dc22

2005015043

10 9 8 7 6 5 4 3 2 1

Published by Sterling Publishing Co., Inc.
387 Park Avenue South, New York, NY 10016

Distributed in Canada by Sterling Publishing
c/o Canadian Manda Group, 165 Dufferin Street
Toronto, Ontario, Canada M6K 3H6
Distributed in the United Kingdom by GMC Distribution Services
Castle Place, 166 High Street, Lewes, East Sussex, England BN7 1XU
Distributed in Australia by Capricorn Link (Australia) Pty. Ltd.
P. O. Box 704, Windsor, NSW 2756, Australia

Printed and Bound in China

Sterling ISBN-13: 978-1-4027-1921-9 (hardcover)
ISBN-10: 1-4027-1921-3

Sterling ISBN-13: 978-1-4027-5387-9 (paperback)
ISBN-10: 1-4027-5387-X

For information about custom editions, special sales, premium and corporate purchases, please contact Sterling Special Sales Department at 800-805-5489 or specialsales@sterlingpublishing.com.

whenever
possible
skip
rather
than
walk

dedication

Heartfelt gratitude to the special people who helped to make this book possible. Sincere thanks to my agents, John Leonhardt and Julia Dvorin of Panic Entertainment Groupe, Art Institute Glitter, Inc., Making Memories, the imaginative team at All Night Media brand at Plaid Enterprises, and Meryl Taylor at C. R. Gibson.

Janny Stevenson, Barbara Pence, Connie Funk, and Anne Olwin offered sisterly encouragement throughout. I truly appreciate my sons, my daughter, nieces, and nephews for allowing me to use their photos liberally. Thanks to my husband, Russell, whose kindness and patience have proven to be endless.

THE BRIDE
HER WEDDING BO
The BRIDES BOOK of RECIPES AND HOUSEHOLD HINTS

fairy girl
her eyes twinkle brightly
her lips red as cherries
nose turned up so sweetly
feet swift as fairies

contents

a brief history of paper cutting

The magic of paper cutting began so long ago and so far away that it was almost another world entirely. In the courts of imperial China in the second century, paper was a new invention that fascinated the royals, who cut designs for screens, fabric stencils, and embroidery patterns. A new art form was born.

Cutting paper has captivated people in every generation since then. From the Mayan Indians to Muslims decorating the walls of a mosque, from famous storyteller Hans Christian Anderson to the Jewish people hidden away during the Nazi era, this craft has found a home in the hearts of people who had little else in common.

In the sixteenth century, a paper cutters' guild flourished in Turkey. Across Asia, people used cut paper in the production of fabrics, furniture, and even shadow puppet plays. In Europe, cut paper was all the rage for centuries; ladies cut images of home and hearth and shepherds in the Alps cut silhouettes by firelight, using their sheep shears.

In Poland, sheepskins were cut for window coverings, and wycinanka, a traditional style of brightly colored layered paper collage, was born. The Dutch used their cut paper to decorate religious and legal documents, and Jewish marriage contracts, or ketubah, which featured outstanding paper cuts of symbolic religious images.

When the Europeans began to colonize the New World, they brought their paper-cutting traditions with them, capturing the likenesses of loved ones in the era before photography began. Itinerant silhouette artists roamed the Eastern U.S. much like muralists, stencil artists, and portrait painters did.

Because cutting paper requires only the simplest materials, it has been the art form of people who had art in their souls but lacked canvases, brushes, and other expensive supplies. The day I cut my first piece of paper, I had only a Swiss army knife scissors and a lunch bag. That was enough. I am only one of millions of people across the reaches of time and distance who simply love a nice sheet of paper and smile at the thought of what can be done with it.

Whether you're a paper fanatic already or a newcomer to paper arts, if you've always longed to find the magic of hand-cut paper for yourself, this book will be a handy jumping-off guide.

Cut it out!

Sharyn Sowell

Sharyn Sowell

You can't trust your eyes if your imagination's out of focus

general information

the bare-bones basics

You need very little to begin cutting paper. Here are the essentials.

Ordinary office-type scissors — Make certain the scissors you select are sharp and make clean cuts. If you prefer using a craft knife, you'll need a small yet sturdy knife with plenty of blades and a self-healing cutting mat.

Transfer paper — If you want to use patterns, transfer paper or carbon paper is the fastest way to trace a pattern onto your project paper. Fabric stores carry transfer papers made for fabrics; they work just as well on paper. You can make your own transfer paper by heavily scribbling with a pencil onto a sheet of paper. Use a pencil with the softest lead you can find.

Assortment of acid-free papers — Keep your eyes open for bargains and special pieces of paper in every size, color, and weight. Just make certain they're acid-free. If your budget is limited, start with your favorite colors in text weight and cover stock. Steer clear of newsprint and construction papers since they're not acid-free. Don't toss out your scraps, since even small pieces of paper can be used for little projects.

Adhesives — You can use anything from basic white glue to glue sticks, PVA book glues, or craft glues and pastes. Again, the caution is to use only acid-free materials. Rubber cement and other high-acid adhesives can ruin hours of work. Look for glues and pastes that are thick, not runny or watery. Tiny dots of white glue can be effective, but the high-water content can sometimes cause delicate papers to buckle.

That's all you really need to begin. One of the nicest things about cutting paper is the freedom of an art form that requires only a few simple, inexpensive tools and materials.

nice but not essential

If you want to expand your selection of tools and materials, you can go wild and amass a collection of wonderful materials and great tools. Here are some of the items I consider favorites.

Vintage papers and ephemera — Use family photographs (yours or those you can find at garage sales or thrift shops), old letters and diaries, bits of ribbon, old tickets, programs, labels, and books. Look for sheet music, bottle tops, buttons, fabric—anything relatively flat and charmingly aged.

Assorted scissors — While you can cut paper using a basic pair of scissors, you'll likely want several different types for different projects. Embroidery scissors work wonderfully for most of the projects found in this book, but you may also choose decoupage or iris scissors for more precise cutting. See "Choosing the Proper Cutting Tool" on page 12 for details.

Acid-buffering spray — This spray neutralizes the acid found in many vintage papers, forming a coating that helps to stop deterioration and protect the papers surrounding those with the high-acid content. Bottles of neutralizer can be found in most craft supply stores.

Bone folder — Readily available in craft and paper specialty stores, this folding tool is long and flat and helps you create a smooth crisp fold.

Straightedge or ruler — An inexpensive see-through ruler is most versatile. The thin clear plastics with multiple lines across the ruler are my favorites. These are durable, useful, and downright cheap.

Paper storage — For the true paper enthusiast, a storage system that keeps the paper flat and dry is essential. Large, flat under-the-bed plastic containers work well, and because they fit under a bed, they are convenient if you're pressed for space. If you're handy, you can use plywood to build a cabinet with wide flat shelves. Ready-made flat file cabinets are available online and through art supply stores. You may even be lucky enough find them, as I have, in a friend's barn or at an industrial auction.

Other irresistible materials include eyelets and eyelet-crimping tools, hole punches, glitter (especially the superfine ones and colorless sparkly diamond dust), and plastic drafting templates in various-sized circles, ovals, and squares. Some people find they can't live without rhinestones, feathers, dried flowers, leaves and bark, stray bits of leather, pierces and punches, watercolors, and copperplate calligraphy nibs and inks. Many of these things are probably already in your scrapbooking and cardmaking collection. They're all great fun, but you really only need scissors or a craft knife, and a cutting mat, and an ordinary piece of paper to get started.

choosing the proper cutting tool

Some people prefer scissors, some a craft knife. If you haven't cut paper before, you'll likely want to experiment with both.

"What kind of scissors do I need?" you're wondering. "What have you got stashed in the kitchen drawer?" might be my reply. You can start with anything that will cut.

However, to get into those pesky little areas, you'll want something small. Embroidery, decoupage, or surgical scissors work just fine. A well-stocked craft or fabric store should have several ideal, affordable choices. Look for a pair with handles that fit your fingers comfortably, sharply pointed tips, and quality construction. Blunt tips won't be able to poke into tiny interior areas. Medical supply stores carry straight iris scissors, used by ophthalmologists, which work well for tiny precise cuts. Iris scissors also come in a bent variety, but I can't imagine trying to cut paper with them. Fancy-shaped scissors are easy on the budget and lots of fun for decorative edges. Rotary cutting wheels in a variety of styles can make cutting very rapid but work best on long straight cuts.

For those who prefer a knife, you'll want the basic craft knife and a generous supply of blades. Cutting with a dull blade or one that's lost its sharp tip is a fast way to frustration. The other essential tool for cutting with a knife is a self-healing cutting mat. This is a soft plastic mat that goes under the paper and serves as a base for the knife to rest on as you cut.

TIPS FOR CUTTING WITH SCISSORS

This is fun and easier than you might think. Start with any outside line and work your way around the design. It doesn't matter which way you do it. You don't need a system. When you're ready to do the interior areas, simply pierce the tips of your scissors into the paper and make a tiny snip. Press the scissors down into that wee little hole and make another snip. Now you've got a nice opening. Continue cutting according to the pattern.

Use your scissors in the way that works best for you. Practice will tell you what that is, but here's how I do it.

When I'm cutting long strokes, I like to use my favorite scissors—a pair of cheap old scissors from my mother's kitchen drawer. Shorter strokes and piercing into interior areas are done with the more pointed scissors with smaller blades.

TIPS FOR CUTTING WITH A CRAFT KNIFE

Place the self-healing cutting mat on a sturdy table under the paper you intend to cut, and use a smooth stroke to cut from one end of a line on the pattern to the other.

Curves are more difficult to cut with a craft knife than straight lines. When cutting a curve with a knife, try turning the knife slowly and gradually. Don't press too deeply into the cutting mat; you only need to press hard enough to penetrate the paper. You'll want a large supply of extra blades, since a dull one will not cut smoothly, giving poor results. Be extra cautious when using a knife.

a note about paper

Selection of the proper paper to suit the project is important. Acid-free high-quality papers are available in a wide variety of weights.

You'll notice that the heavier and stiffer the paper, the more difficult it will be to cut, regardless of the cutting implement. When you're cutting intricate pieces, especially those that are fairly large, you'll find a fairly lightweight paper more cooperative. If the paper needs stiffening, gluing it to a stiffer backing paper when you're finished is a good solution.

Don't limit yourself to papers labeled for scrapbooking or cardmaking, or things precut to standard sizes. I love 12" x 12" solid color papers—the full-size sheets are irresistible. You can slice them up into anything you like. Watercolor and pastel papers are terrific, and even gift wrap, waxed paper, and tracing paper work well. Don't neglect to shop in the fine-art aisle where you will find treasures galore.

Keep your eyes open; great paper is all around us. My son works in the produce department of our local grocery store. One day when shopping, I found him unpacking boxes of pears. There was the most wonderful paper separating the layers of fruit. What a glorious shade of purpley blue. I just had to have it! Of course, my son began to save it for me, and after a liberal spray of acid neutralizer, that paper turned into some pretty fine backgrounds.

how to use the patterns

The patterns in this book are versatile, and you'll want to change size, color, and even shape to fit the project you've got in mind. Simply use a photocopy machine to enlarge or reduce the pattern as necessary. Hold the pattern up to your envelope or scrapbook and adjust the size as necessary.

Next, transfer the pattern onto the back of the paper you plan to cut. Do not apply a pattern to the front of the paper, as lines may be visible on the finished project. Begin by placing your transfer paper, reproducing side down, onto your project paper. Place the photocopied pattern on top of the transfer paper and firmly but gently go over the lines, using a pencil or ballpoint pen. You can also use the pattern as a general guide and sketch the lines on lightly with a pencil, or cut without first drawing the pattern.

Using scissors or a craft knife and self-healing cutting mat, cut out the design and assemble.

cutting letters

You'll notice the alphabet patterns are shown backward. This is important, because you'll trace them onto the back of the sheet of paper. You also must trace the letters right to left instead of left to right, for the same reason. When you look at the finished product, you'll be looking at the reverse of what you traced. Before cutting, you can check to make sure everything's right by holding the paper up to a mirror. What you see in the mirror will be the way the cut-out letters will look.

cutting without a pattern

Maybe you're like me. Maybe just looking at a pattern makes you say, "You're not my mother! I don't have to do what you say!" Bingo. Strike out on your own and leave that pattern behind. Here's how I do it.

Imagination and visualization are the keys to success when you're cutting freehand. Spend some time planning the design in your head. Plan carefully where the various design elements will touch one another. These are crucial since you'll need to join the separate parts of the design at these joints; if you forget this, your design will be a collection of tiny pieces instead of a cohesive piece of paper.

Cutting freehand isn't easy. It takes longer to master but can be infinitely satisfying. You don't imitate anyone else; you define your own style and follow your own muse. No two pieces turn out the same and the more you cut, the better you become. It's the ultimate in paper-cutting artistry.

Ready to try? Start simple with this exercise. Any sort of paper will do. An old magazine or telephone book is a great source for practice paper, and since you're going to throw it away, quality isn't an issue.

Imagine in your mind a simple teapot like the one below. Pick up the scissors and paper and begin cutting at the spout. Cut up and around the lid, turning the paper as you go. Cut down to and around the handle. Don't worry about the inside of the handle yet. Cut down to and around the base, then back up to the spout to finish. Pierce your scissors into what will be the center of the teapot's handle hole. Make a tiny cut; then slip your scissors into that opening and snip your way around the handle hole.

It's likely that your first attempts will be terribly disproportioned and lopsided. Don't be alarmed. Don't give up. Everyone starts this way. It's the beginning of the learning curve. Try the exercise over again, checking to see where you went wrong and doing it a little better the next time. You'll notice yourself improving a little each time.

Even the most basic shapes are charming when you turn them into a sweet little card or scrapbook decoration. I used the teapot exercise to make this birthday card for my sister.

When you're ready, try other simple shapes. Leaves, simple buildings, or a child's profile are all good choices for beginning freehand cutting. Even if you decide to use patterns most of the time, this is a wonderful exercise for eye and hand, and you'll learn much about proportion, scale, line, and form.

When cutting freehand, it's important to remember that art is an experience and the results don't have to be splendid. It's not about producing a perfect product, but about enjoyment and learning. Enjoy yourself and don't worry about botched results. Toss them in the trash and keep on cutting.

positive & negative space

When asked how he formed his sculpture of David, Michelangelo said that he simply removed from the marble anything that didn't look like David. Cutting paper has many similarities to sculpture. With most arts, one adds something to form an image. With paper cutting and sculpture, it's what we remove that forms the image one sees. That's positive space, and it's what most of us think of when we cut paper.

An understanding of positive and negative space becomes crucial. There are only two ways to form an image from the paper. When you use positive space, you cut away everything that is not part of the image you want your viewer to see. When you use negative space, it's what you remove that forms the image. I love negative space because it allows me to think backward, to form images from what "isn't there." Sometimes you will want to use one, sometimes the other, sometimes both. It's important to think about positive and negative space and how they play off one another.

You'll find both positive and negative images in the patterns that follow.

An easy exercise will help explain positive and negative space better than my words could ever do. Grab a pair of scissors and a sheet of paper. Any sort and size of paper will do.

Cut a simple pattern in the paper, like a circle or a star. On the left-hand side of the table, lay the original piece of paper. On the right, lay the piece you cut out. The image you see on your left is the negative; the one on the right is the positive.

Of the thousands of sheets I've cut, my favorites are those that include both positive and negative space effectively. One way to include both positive and negative in one image is the technique described above. I did this when I designed my business logo—my favorite pair of scissors.

a few things to remember

It's only a piece of paper. My neighbor paints her house the most gorgeous and brilliant colors. About every six months she'll choose a different shade of emerald or scarlet or sky blue. When I gasp and ask her how she has the nerve to try this latest hue, she laughs and says, "It's only paint."

Michelle, my hairdresser, tells me to try a new hairstyle. "Why not?" she asks. "It'll grow. It's only hair."

Now it's my turn to say it my way. Have an idea? Try it. Let your imagination go wild. Why not? It's only paper.

Be safe. Be careful with your cutting tools. It may seem silly, but my mother was right when she said, "Safety first." You don't want yourself or your child or pet to be the victim of an accidental cut.

I know what I'm talking about. My dog chewed on the mat-cutter handle and barely missed the blade. What on earth was I thinking? Be smarter than I was and keep tools out of reach of children and pets.

Have fun. Don't take yourself too seriously. We're cutting for fun, not frustration. If a project is difficult and giving you fits, look for ways to simplify the piece and enjoy it. If a project turns out poorly, toss it out with a laugh. You can try the same thing again or go on to something you'll like better. This is meant to be pure pleasure, not a competition.

Make your own rules. Because I have never had an instructor and have always cut everything freehand, I cut just as I like. You can cut on a whim, too. Use a pattern, change the patterns, or leave them out entirely. Do the fiddly bits first, or do them last. Cut top to bottom if you like, or bottom to top. There's no right or wrong way. There are no rules, and you can cut what you like the way you like. If you don't like it, toss it out and start again. It's only paper.

Use high-quality materials. It doesn't have to be expensive, but you really must use good-quality materials. Some people have invested a wealth of time in a project only to have it deteriorate because they used rubber cement, construction paper, and other inferior materials. Value yourself enough to use quality paper and adhesives. After all, these may turn into family heirlooms one day.

Create your own patterns. The patterns in this book are for your personal use and enjoyment. Cut as many as you like for your family and seven hundred of your closest friends, but please don't sell a single one. Not only is it illegal to sell products you made from a copyrighted pattern, but you'll feel so much better if you sell designs that came only from your imagination.

Additionally, these patterns are only meant to be a jumping-off spot. Change them any way you like or use them just for ideas. Don't be afraid to experiment. After all, it's only a piece of paper. Try out your own ideas; that's how we learn. If you don't like the results, you can toss it in the trash and begin again.

Take the plunge. When I began to cut paper, I cut my way through a towering stack of telephone books and never saved a single sheet. By the time I finished those phone books, I'd become a hard-core scissor addict. Don't be afraid to join me in the ranks of people who will cut out anything, and trash it just as quickly. It's only a piece of paper, and you can save it as an heirloom or add it to the garbage pile, all on a whim.

Now, it's time to pick up those scissors and begin.

classic greeting cards

You'll find that many of the patterns shown in other sections of the book will adapt perfectly for cards, but here are a few specially planned to make imaginative hand-cut greetings.

The method for creating most greeting cards is the same.

YOU'LL NEED:

- Assorted glitters, beads, markers, and other goodies to decorate your cards (optional)
- Background paper for card and an envelope to fit card
- Glue or glue stick
- Paper

HERE'S HOW:

1. Cut a piece of paper to fit your background paper, allowing extra room for a fold-over at the top, if included in your pattern.
2. Trace the pattern or draw your own version on the back of the paper.
3. Cut out the design.
4. Embellish the design if you like with glitter, beads, etc.
5. Glue the design to the card.

lattice rose

This charming card is one for a special person's special occasion. It's rather challenging and not something I'd recommend for a beginner. Getting the tiny cuts and curves smooth and flowing is time consuming, but the results speak for themselves.

See Lattice Rose Pattern on page 96.

garden delights

Sometimes you want something small to decorate a little space. Use these little garden-inspired patterns to jump-start your own creativity. Gift enclosure cards, notepapers, or matching gift wraps work well with small patterns like these. Try your hand at simple shapes that can be easily cut without using a pattern; soon you'll be snipping out everything from butterflies to sand dollars.

See Garden Delights Pattern on page 99.

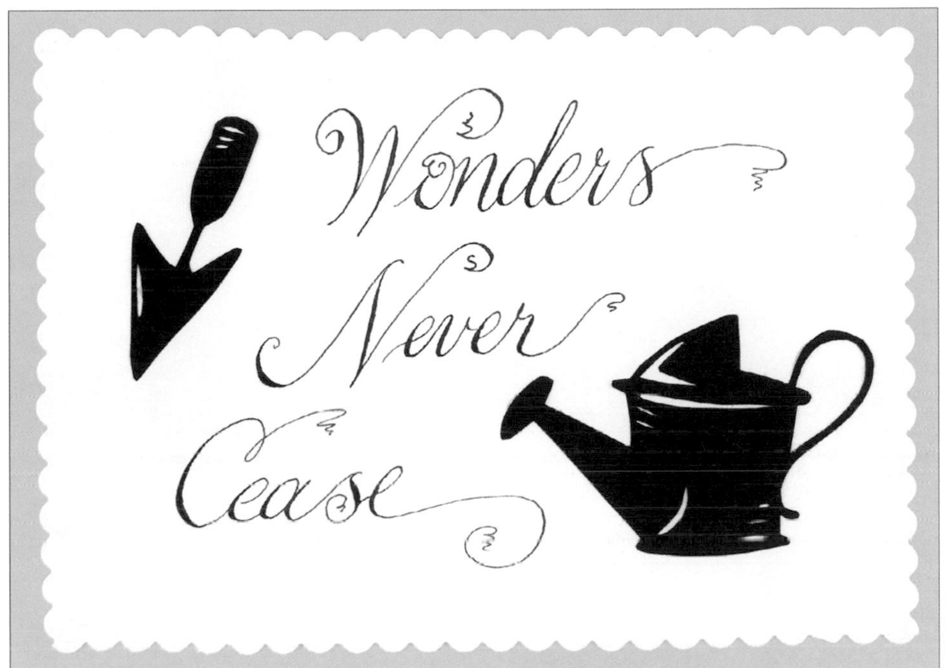

little house

This tiny image makes a nice card for almost any occasion.

See Little House Pattern on page 105.

the flower basket

This pattern is a bit more difficult than most, requiring patience and a steady hand. It makes a nice Mother's Day, wedding, or birthday card, and you can easily adjust the size to fit your paper or envelope.

See The Flower Basket Pattern on page 102.

gardener's delight

It's easy to alter this pattern if you want a woman instead of a man. Add hair at the back of the head and make the brim a bit wider.

See Gardener's Delight Pattern on page 100.

Tips & Tricks

Embellishments for Cards

You may notice that most of my cards include layered papers for depth, but few 3-D embellishments. That's because when you're mailing a card that will go through mechanical equipment in transit, it's safer not to include anything that can be damaged. I embellish with glitter, glue, stamps, and other flat materials; but when I'm mailing a card, I omit anything fragile.

fairy girls

What could be more charming than this dear piece? Two fairy girls offer dainty bouquets to one another. This design works well cut in almost any color that contrasts well with its background.

See Fairy Girls Pattern on page 98.

Tips & Tricks

Folding with the Paper's Grain

Like fabric and wood, paper has a direction. Similar to fabric's warp and weft, if you cut enough paper, you'll find that it isn't the same both ways. Folding with the grain of the paper is much easier than folding against the grain.

To determine the direction of the paper's grain, lay a sheet parallel to the table and let a fixed amount (I use 6") hang over. Observe how far the paper droops. Now rotate the paper 90 degrees and let it hang over by the same amount. Observe the droop in the paper again. The direction in which the paper droops further will fold far more smoothly and easily.

witchy halloween

Just the thing if you like to send Halloween greetings. You can enlarge this card for a window decoration, too. It's easy enough for a beginner.

See Witchy Halloween Pattern on page 114.

lined cutout cards

Put a little spin on the classic greeting card by making a lined cutout card like one of the Winter Mittens shown below. Vary your card selection by using other simple shapes for the body of the card such as stars, pine trees, houses, etc.

YOU'LL NEED:

- Cardstock folded to 5" x 7" card
- Contrasting color paper for liner
- Envelopes to fit the card
- Glitter (optional)
- Glue or glue stick

HERE'S HOW:

1. Trace the pattern for the card shape on the back of the card and cut out.
2. Cut a liner just a bit smaller than the card shape.
3. With a pencil, very lightly trace one of the patterns for the card design or draw a simple design (tree, deer, stars, zig-zags) on the inside front of the card and cut out.
4. Glue the liner to the inside front of card.
5. If you like glitter, add some to simulate sparkling snow.

winter mittens

What a charmingly simple project! Because it's fast, it's a good choice for a batch of holiday cards or invitations to an afternoon of snowman-building and cocoa.

See Winter Mittens Card Pattern and Winter Mittens #1–#3 Patterns on pages 116–117.

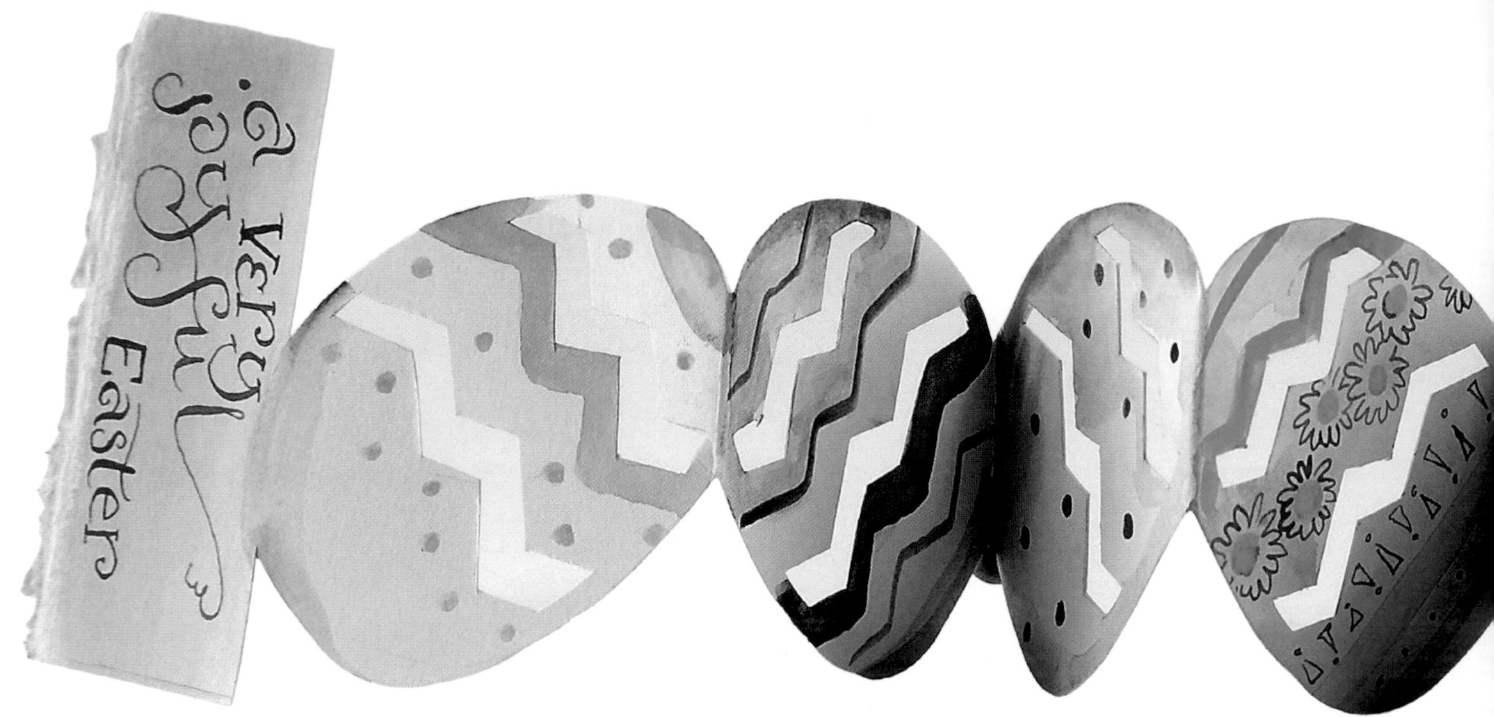

paper chain cards

Paper chain cards such as Joyful Easter, Hand-painted Teacup, Skipping Time, and From One Nut on pages 29–31 are variations on that old and dearly beloved occupation of cutting paper dolls. You can adjust the sizes and use them across the page or cut them into segments and assemble them into frames.

Many of the other patterns in the book can be turned into paper chains simply by cutting the patterns in repetition, and you can easily make up your own designs. The simpler the better, however, when it comes to paper chains. Don't attempt too many layers at once or you'll have slippage and poor quality.

YOU'LL NEED:

- Crayons, markers, or watercolors (optional)
- Glue or glue stick
- Paper

HERE'S HOW:

1. Measure the height and width of the design you want to use. Cut the paper into a long strip just a bit longer in height than the design.
2. Accordion-fold the paper into the width you'll be using. Note: You can glue segments of paper end-to-end to achieve the desired length.
3. Trace or draw the pattern on the top layer of the folded paper.
4. Cut out the design. I recommend cutting no more than three layers at a time, and I frequently cut only one thickness of paper at a time.
5. Retrace the pattern as needed and repeat the procedure until the chain is as long as you like.
6. Decorate using crayons, markers, or watercolors.

joyful easter

Decorating this card was as much fun as decorating real easter eggs. I used white watercolor paper and bright washes of watercolor paints. I embellished the washes with familiar patterns of polka dots, swirls, stripes, and stars. You can personalize the tabs of the card, using a fine-tipped paintbrush or marker.

See Joyful Easter Pattern on page 97.

hand-painted teacup

This charming teacup can be decorated to suit almost any occasion or sentiment. Here, it is used to communicate longing in the absence of a dear friend. It would also make a delightful invitation to an afternoon tea.

See Hand-painted Teacup Pattern on page 97.

skipping time

Reminiscent of cutting simple paper dolls, this cheerful pattern is slighty more complex yet definitely more appealing to the eye. See open Skipping Time card on page 3.

See Skipping Time Pattern on page 97.

from one nut

Paper chains that contain a personalized message create excitement for the receiver since the entire message is unknown until the last fold is revealed.

See From One Nut Pattern on page 97.

Tips & Tricks

Alternative Uses

If you have so much fun with paper chains that you don't want to stop when your cards and scrapbooks are finished, let me whisper the suggestion that these look fabulous tacked to the edges of a shelf, hung on the Christmas tree, swinging along with crepe paper as birthday decorations, or even elongated, enlarged, and layered to make a pair of curtains.

accordion-fold cards

It's easy to make a special little accordion-fold card or book like Field Flowers and Girl Skipping with two small pieces of cardboard, a ribbon, and a long strip of paper. Remember, you can decorate both sides of an accordion-fold book.

YOU'LL NEED:

- Decorative paper
- Embellishments such as contrasting color paper (optional)
- Long strip of paper
- Two 4" squares of lightweight cardboard

HERE'S HOW:

1. Cover the cardboard with decorative paper.
2. Count the letters or pages needed in your greeting and accordion-fold the strip of long paper into the same number of folds, adding two extra folds. Note: One of the extra folds will be attached to the front cover and one to the back.
3. Using a pencil, lightly trace a greeting onto the back of the folded paper. I sometimes use one letter for each square. Note: If you draw your own letters, remember to do them backward. If you want alphabet patterns, you'll find some on pages 119–123.
4. Cut out the letters or patterns.
5. If you like, you can leave them as is, or if you prefer a bright color, you can cut small pieces of lighter weight paper with decorative-edged scissors and glue them behind each letter.
6. Glue the end pages to the cardboard, placing the ribbon under the back page. Let dry thoroughly, fold up, and tie with the ribbon.

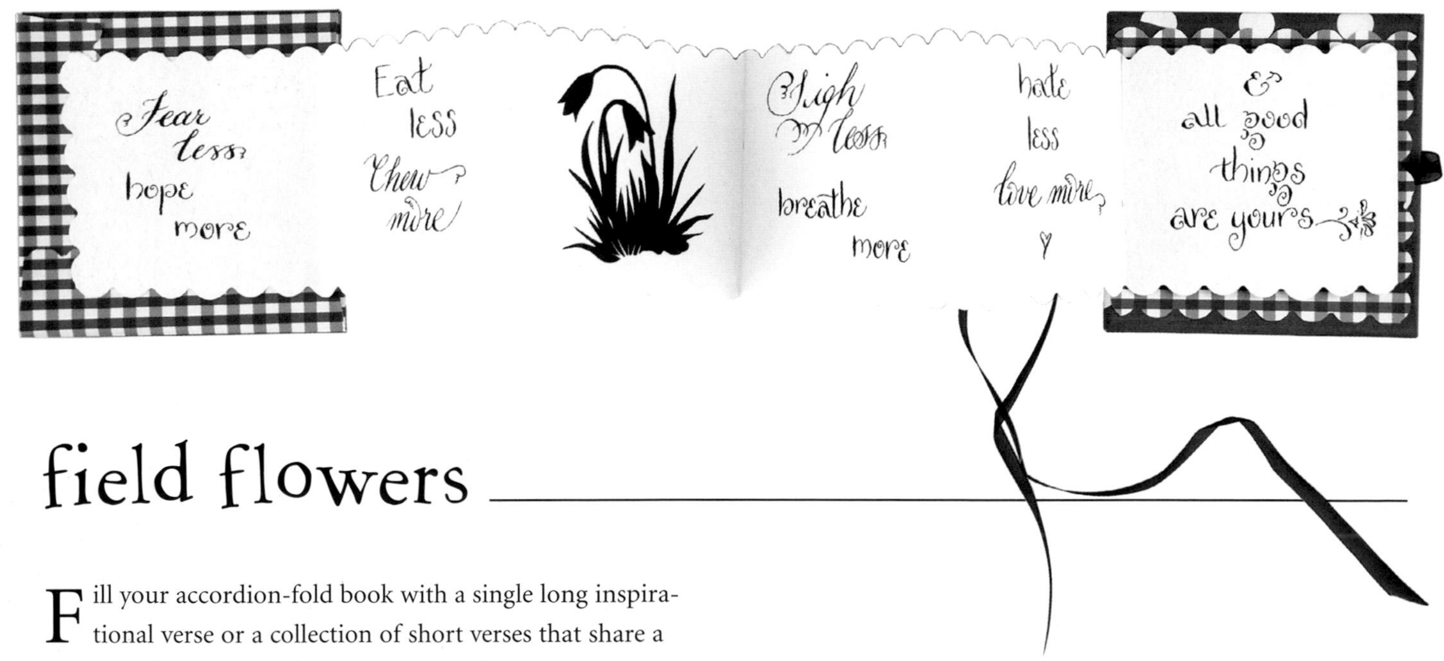

field flowers

Fill your accordion-fold book with a single long inspirational verse or a collection of short verses that share a common theme. A cut image completes the book.

See Field Flowers Pattern on page 97.

whenever
possible
skip
rather
than
walk

girl skipping

The whimsical image in this accordion-fold book is paired with a matching verse and capped with pink polka-dot and floral patterned paper covers.

See Girl Skipping Pattern on page 97.

LEMON
rather
than
walk
whenever
possible
skip

Tips & Tricks

Making Smoother Folds

Use a bone folder to make folding the flaps easier and more crisp and flat. Lay your paper upside down and place a straightedge along a fold line. With the tip pointing down, run the bone folder alongside the straightedge, pressing gently but firmly. Now bend, and voila! A straight, smooth fold.

December
Ho! Ho! Ho!
Merry Christmas!

scrapbooks & journals

When you're thinking about cut paper for scrapbooks, a little advance planning can help you avoid layouts that don't work well. Assemble the photos you'll be using for your page along with background papers; then select a design that matches the theme of your photos. Now is the time to decide whether you want the soft look of a pastel, the punch of a brilliant color, or the bold drama of black.

At this point I always make a tentative layout, then determine how much space I want the cut paper to take up. I measure the available space so I know how much room I have to play with. Avoid trying to fit too much on a page; you'll end up with a distracting mess. It's better to balance cut paper, photos, lettering and embellishments so the end result is both interesting and restful to the eye.

chocoholic

Being a devoted chocoholic, I decided to ask my friends for their favorite chocolate recipes. I'll glue them into this little booklet along with the contributors' photos. Something like this would make a memorable bridal shower or birthday gift.

See Chocoholic Pattern on page 123.

stylish woman

Curvaceous and bold, this woman is all about chic style. I accentuated the slightly retro flavor of the design by incorporating some '40s flash cards I bought at a tag sale. Paired with a photo of my grandma and Aunt Susie, the image gives an updated look to a heritage page.

See Stylish Woman Pattern on page 108.

black dress, glove & heels

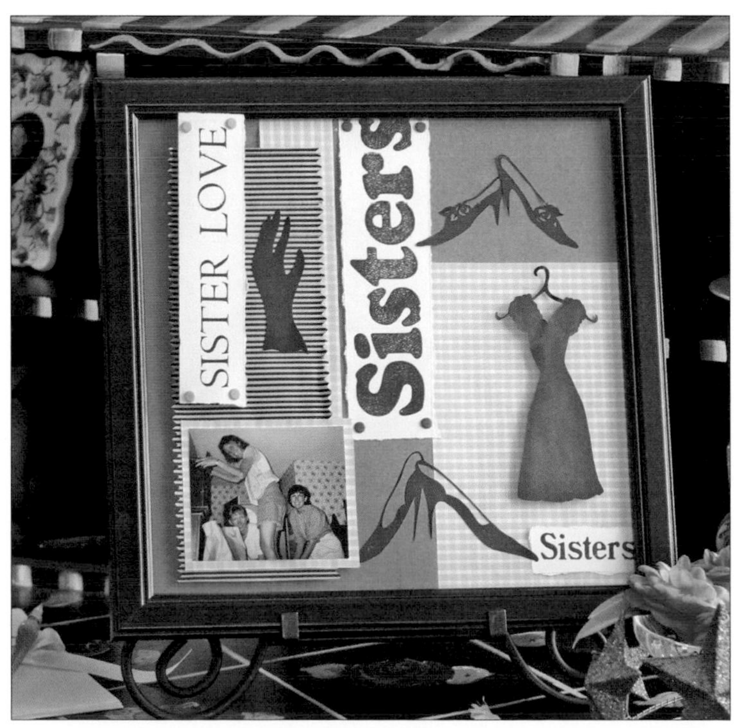

My sisters and I faithfully take an annual sisters' retreat, which always produces plenty of photos that need to be included in my scrapbook. This page includes one photo and four chic cutouts. Like many of my other pages, this one pairs unusual colors and patterns. It's fun to break conventional rules.

See Black Dress Pattern, Glove Pattern, and Heels Patterns on page 110.

gone fishing

I live with diehard fishermen so I decorate lots of fishing pages. These fun fish are quick and easy to cut. The air bubbles are acrylic rhinestones.

See Gone Fishing Pattern on page 109.

flip-flop heaven

If you're a fan of the ever-popular flip-flops, this is the pattern for you. Use a large flip-flop alone for a fast and very easy summer-day scrapbook page, card, or journal page. A series of patterns in smaller sizes will frame your summertime photographs very nicely.

See Flip-flop Heaven Pattern on page 98.

peaceful birds on a branch

This piece gently highlights a photograph or paragraph without enclosing it. Outdoor themes like this one complement the serenity of nature in a photograph. This design works well in almost any natural color.

See Peaceful Birds on a Branch Pattern on page 109.

the cradle

A dear little cradle under a bower of blooms to welcome a special child. For the page shown, I cut the cradle in two sizes and elevated them with slivers of foam-board to emphasize the delicate nature of both the baby and the cut paper.

See The Cradle Pattern on page 103.

spring bouquet

Try this in black, white, or a pastel shade for that feeling of spring. Reduced in size, this design makes a lovely card.

See Spring Bouquet Pattern on page 101.

aspen

Use your surroundings to inspire cut-paper designs. Trees and leaves abound with eye-catching shapes that are easy to mimic in paper. When we made our annual trek to the family cabin in the woods, I couldn't get enough of cutting maple, aspen, and poplar leaves. Try this simple pattern to get you started.

See Aspen Pattern on page 108.

swans in a heart

Romantic and sentimental, this design has a traditional feel. Notice how the swans were elevated on tiny bits of foam-board to give a strong sense of dimension.

See Swans in a Heart Pattern on page 100.

jack-o'-lanterns

We have never done a scary Halloween at our house, preferring silly faces like this funny pumpkin instead.

Don't forget, you can use a pattern in many different ways. I change the size of the pumpkins and use them for both cards and scrapbook pages.

See Jack-o'-lanterns Pattern on page 114.

snow boy & snow girl

Saucy and chilly, this romantic pair will liven up your scrapbook pages. You can enlarge the pattern for a holiday door decoration or reduce it for a card.

I used waxed linen thread to add a simple blanket stitch, suggestive of warm mittens, and some cheerful jingle bells to embellish the happy pair.

See Snow Boy & Snow Girl Patterns on page 115.

December
Ho! Ho! Ho!
Merry Christmas!

(left) santa & his gifts

This jolly Christmas page decoration works well when cut in colors, too. I love vintage papers and often use them in my work. If the paper is precious, scan and print it on your computer or make a color photocopy. Old sheet music seems to be rather plentiful and cheap in thrift stores so I frequently incorporate it into projects like this one.

See Santa & His Gifts Pattern on page 118.

santa's stocking

Try this fanciful fellow in bright red or green, or use traditional black with an heirloom Christmas photograph. I often sprinkle glitter as a highlight on this page without using glue, simply allowing a hint of sparkle to wink from the paper.

See Santa's Stocking Pattern on page 118.

grandma

I know a bank where the wild thyme blows
Where oxlips & the nodding violet grows
Quite over-canopied with luscious woodbine
With sweet musk-roses and with eglantine

fabulous frames

There's nothing nicer than a simple but elegantly framed picture or handwritten greeting. Hand-cut paper can be a particularly charming enhancement to a treasured photograph or a written sentiment. Frames can consist of a simple border cut and mitered to fit, or an elaborate concoction of finely snipped paper.

Most frames, whether simple or incredibly complex, are designs with openings or blank areas for a photograph or words. The instructions for completing the frames that follow are quite straightforward.

YOU'LL NEED:

- Backing paper
- Embellishments such as colored pencils or markers (optional)
- Glue or glue stick
- Paper
- Photograph

HERE'S HOW:

1. Photocopy the pattern or sketch a similar one onto the back of the paper, adjusting to fit the photograph you want to use.
2. Cut out the frame.
3. Crop the photograph to fit the area. You can glue your photograph on top of the frame or cut a hole and glue the photograph behind the frame. Choose the method that works best for your project.
4. Apply glue sparingly to the photograph and carefully ease the photograph into place on or behind the frame. Note: You want barely enough glue to adhere the materials, not so much that the glue oozes out and ruins the entire project.
5. Apply glue evenly to the entire back of the frame. Gently lay the photograph and frame onto the backing paper of your choice and flatten.

rose bush

When you have one special photograph that you want to showcase on a scrapbook page, this design does it with drama. I chose to cut white paper and set it on a black background to frame this cherished black-and-white family photo.

See Rose Bush Pattern on page 102.

Mercy me, darlin'!
This girl's going out on the town!

our town

Miniature houses, fences, trees, and vehicles decorate this frame. Ideal for a neighborhood photograph, this pattern adapts well to a card that would make the perfect "We're moving" announcement.

See Our Town Pattern on page 105.

cupid

Sweet and old-fashioned, this piece was inspired by a photograph from the 1880s. Updated with a bright alphabet, the image goes contemporary; but it looks just as dear when done in vintage or muted tones.

See Cupid Pattern on page 107.

Tips & Tricks

Measure Twice, Cut Once

If you're cutting freehand as I do, the easiest way to make certain your hand-cut paper fits the space is to first cut your paper into a rectangle or oval that fits the space. If you're using a pattern, play with the copier to adjust the size to fit your space. Then when you begin to snip your design, you know you won't end up with a piece that's too large, a common error for beginners.

easter eggs

A merry ring of eggs enclose this springtime photograph. Be careful when cutting the inside of the curves to keep the scissors moving in a gentle curve, not in a jerky abrupt angle. If you find the finished product jagged and rough-looking, watch to see that you're not forcing the scissors through the paper, but instead are feeding it through the blades in a smooth motion that doesn't bend the paper.

See Easter Eggs Pattern on page 112.

sea stars

Because this piece has longer cuts with no abrupt angles, it's an excellent choice for a less experienced paper cutter. I used waxed linen thread to stitch on the shells, making special use of those that already had naturally bored holes.

See Sea Stars Pattern on page 108.

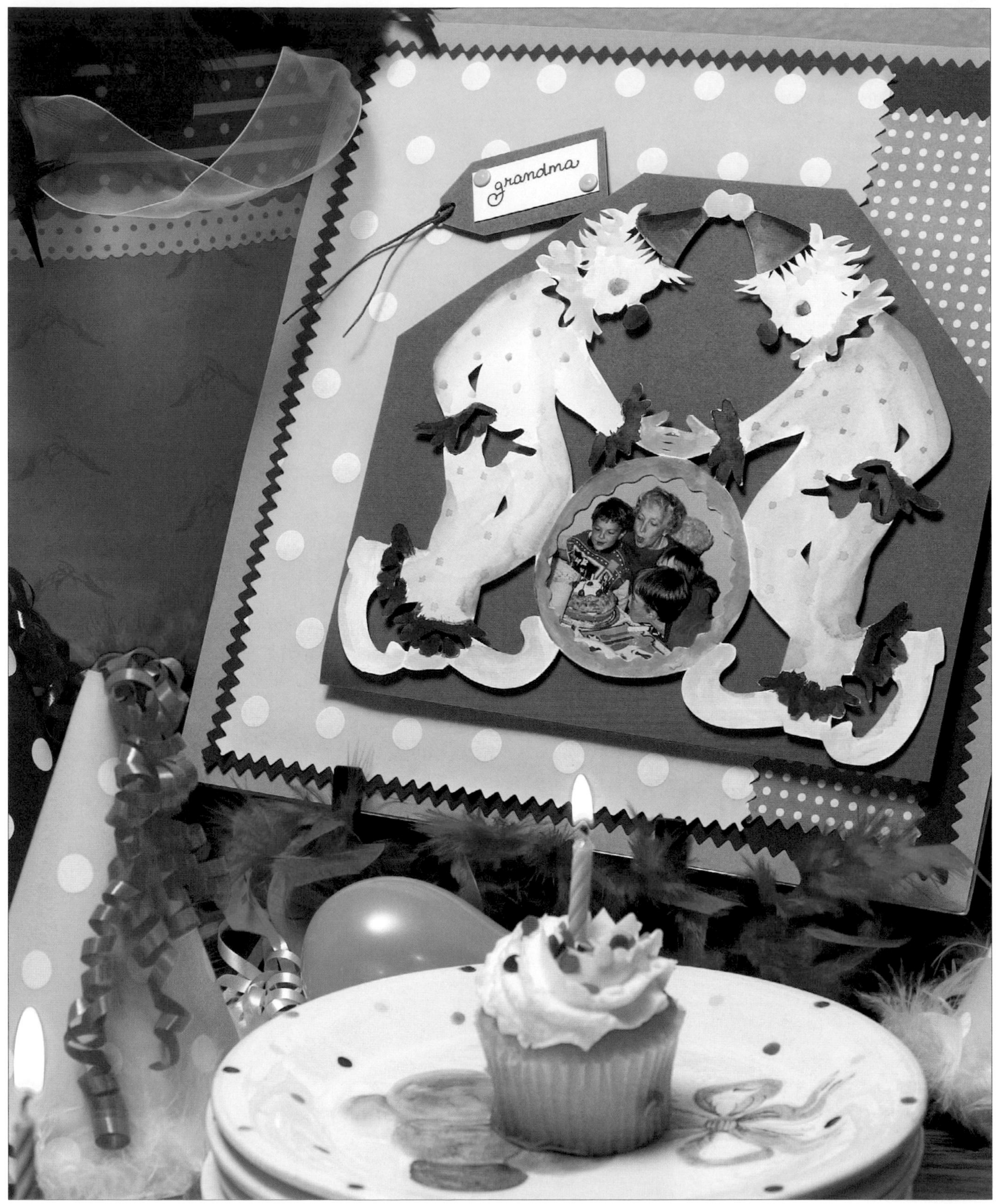
grandma

(left) jolly clowns

I like to use paint or markers in brilliant happy colors for a child's page, but you could do it in almost any solid color. Reduced to card size, these clowns would be a fun invitation.

See Jolly Clowns Pattern on page 112.

Tips & Tricks

Coloring the Cut Paper

One way to make the hand-cut paper really stand out is to add color. Watercolors, markers, glitter, crayons, inks, and dyes are just a few of the possibilities. After you cut the paper, embellish it to your heart's content. For the Birthday Candles scrapbooking page below, I cut the piece from watercolor paper, then used light washes of water-color paints to brighten the candles. The calligraphy was done using a copperplate calligraphy nib and the same watercolor paints.

birthday candles

This frame is perfect for showcasing a photo of the main event at a birthday party—blowing out the candles. The open corner areas provide ample room for journaling.

See Birthday Candles Pattern on page 113.

climbing roses

This project is similar to the Lattice Rose greeting card shown on page 22. Choose a fairly lightweight paper to allow you to manipulate knife or scissors in the tiny areas. I like this design in tone-on-tone or even dramatic black and white.

Be gentle with the tiny areas and pay special attention to the curves. With delicate florals, it's especially important to watch that you don't end up with jagged cuts, but only soft gentle curves.

Here, I've repeated a technique shown earlier, cutting many pieces of foam-board into tiny slivers and gluing on both sides to add a dramatic sense of dimension to the cut paper. The same technique works very effectively if you want to use the piece framed in a shadowbox. Note: Because pages like these are fragile, it's a good idea to enclose them in a plastic sleeve.

See Climbing Roses Pattern on page 104.

(right) flowers & ferns

Victorians believed old-fashioned bleeding hearts, pansies, and ferns signified enduring affection and love. These posies make an exceptional frame for a special photograph or journal entry.

See Flowers & Ferns Pattern on page 104.

Crowds of bees are
giddy with clover
Crowds of grasshoppers
dance at our feet
Crowds of larks at their
matins hang over
Thanking the Lord for
a life so sweet

birdhouses & vines

This frame is versatile enough for almost any photograph, and easily adaptable for a journal page. You can also crop the birds and their houses, leaving a simple trellis that makes a great invitation. Because I collect birds' nests and love everything related to wild birds, I often incorporate the little singers into my work. Feathers soften the design.

See Birdhouses & Vines Pattern on page 112.

Tips & Tricks

Making the Paper Lie Flat

Because paper has a grain, when you cut and handle it, especially in an intricate pattern, it can warp and fold. It just doesn't want to lie nice and flat. However, you can make it behave by ironing it flat. I use an iron from the 1940s, one that hasn't seen a drop of water since long before I was born. It's important not to use a steam iron since even a hint of moisture can wreak havoc with the hand-cut paper. Place the paper wrong side up on an ironing board and set the iron to the lowest heat. Iron it gently, using short rapid strokes. The paper should be flat and ready to glue.

best friends & books

If you would prefer a boy, simply trace the pattern without including the braids or bow. I used a torn and damaged page from a vintage book to decorate the border.

See Best Friends & Books Pattern on page 107.

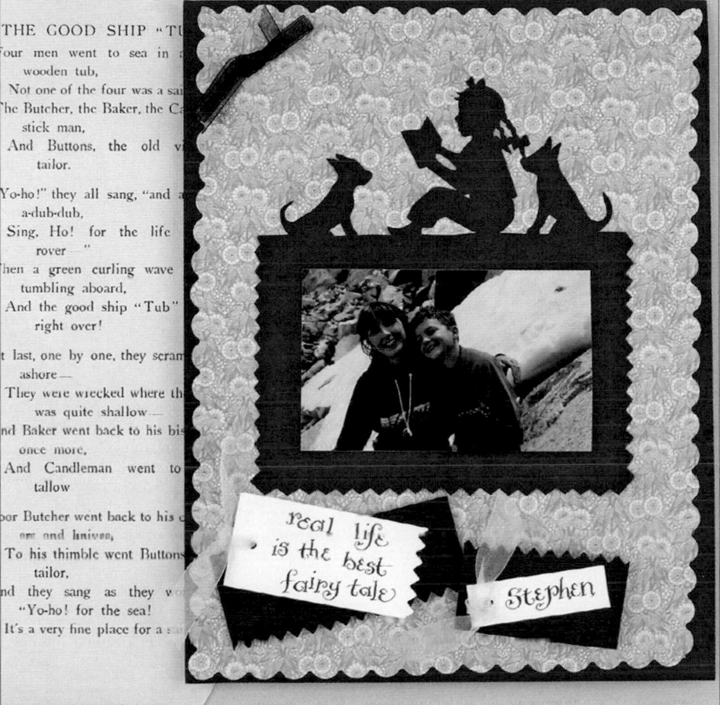

birds on a twig branch

If you're learning to pierce the paper with the tips of your scissors, this project is for you. Because the twigs are rustic, little slips won't be noticeable.

See Birds on a Twig Branch Pattern on page 103.

Tips & Tricks

Using Dimensional Elements

When I include elements that have a lot of dimension and texture, I'm careful to place a simple, heavy cardstock page between scrapbook pages to ensure that they won't take an unwanted imprint. Often, these separation pages are decorated only with a simple caption or poem.

I know a bank where the wild thyme blows
Quite over-canopied with luscious woodbine

rose leaf

Use bold color for a contemporary look, delicate watercolor details for a dainty feeling, or traditional black and white for a vintage flavor.

This Rose Leaf frame shows the same pattern cut two ways. One, above, is a colorful piece, done in greens with tiny red rosebuds, that surrounds a photo of my niece in my garden. The other, at right, done in black and white, accents a heritage page of my Grandma's wedding book.

See Rose Leaf Pattern on page 108.

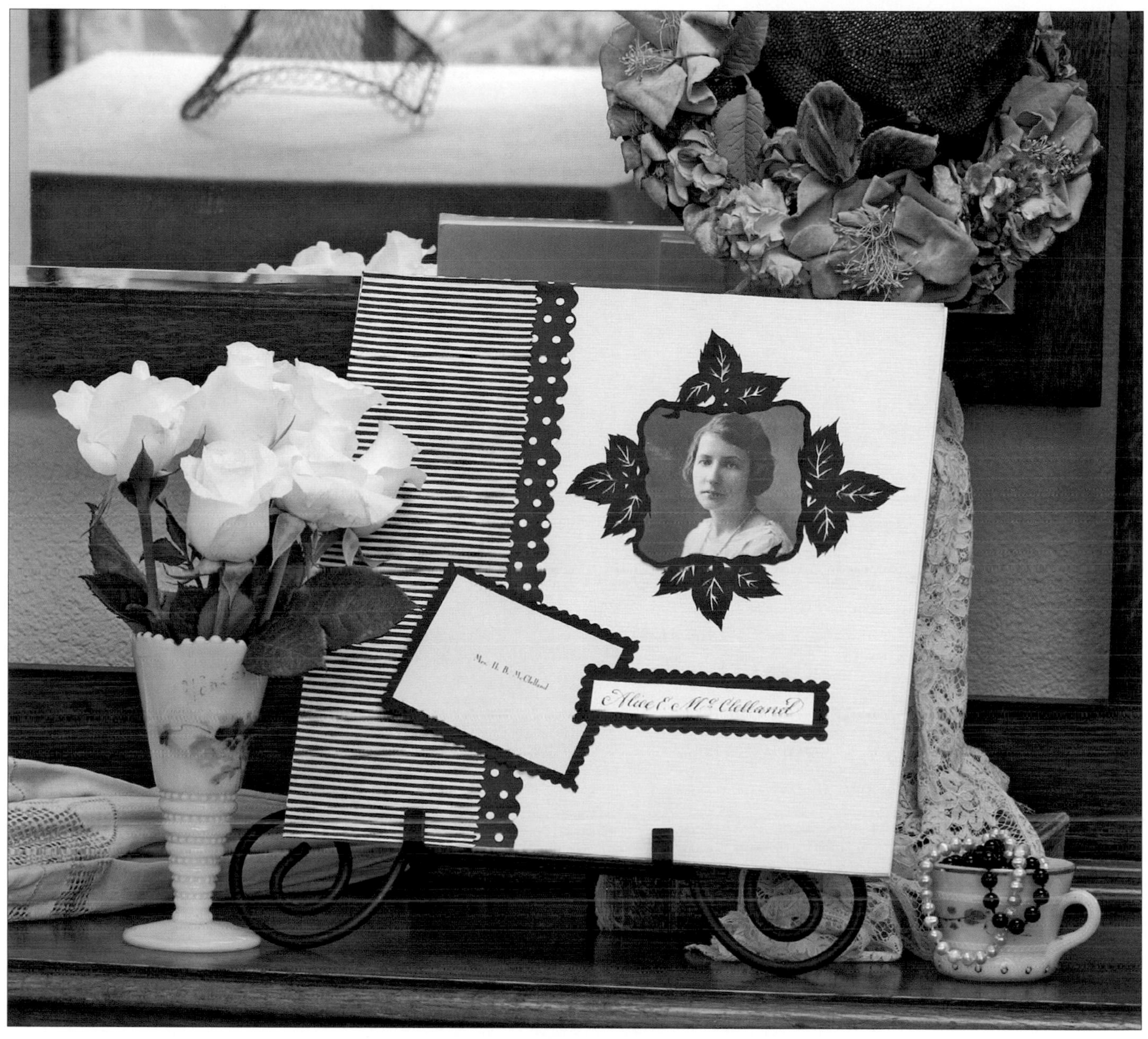

Tips & Tricks

Getting the "Feel" You Want

Before starting a project, I always try to get a very specific mental picture and a definite feel for the look I want to achieve. When you know what you're aiming for, you can tailor the cut paper to suit the piece. You can cut the same piece from different papers and use embellishments and color to change the flavor entirely. The two pieces shown here illustrate how differently the same shape can look.

garden flowers

Tiny pierced holes and sharp curves make this project a challenge. When a design is both intricately dainty and strikingly elemental, I like to keep the elements on the page to a bare minimum, allowing the beauty of the design to emerge without competition.

See Garden Flowers Pattern on page 102.

trick or treat

Cut a hole for a photograph, paste a picture on top of the frame, or use as a journal page.

See Trick or Treat Pattern on page 114.

Tips & Tricks

Chic Storage

I used to be embarrassed about my thrifty ways, my reluctance to part with even a sliver of my favorite gold foil or old book page. When I started hiding them in layers under my toolbox for protection, I realized things had gone too far. It was time to take myself in hand and get control. I stopped being embarrassed and took pride in my ragtag collection, corralling them into one place where I could be more organized.

A small covered cake pan bought at a garage sale, Grandpa's old shirt box, or anything large and flat is a perfect place to stash those precious bits. I always put the prettiest parts face up. If you peeped under the lid of my secret-stash-cake-pan right now, you'd find antique book fragments, a torn piece of sheet music for "America the Beautiful," and wee tiny bits of my favorite French paper in shades of lavender and teal. Also, of course, my own designer paper printed on my computer printer.

Find a reasonably small, charming cast-off with a lid and use it to organize the tiny bits and pieces you can't resist saving.

Easter Finery
Fancy suspenders & a spiffy
green coat. Oh my!
Aren't we the
coolest cousins on the block!

beautiful borders

Decorative borders include any treatment that rings the edges of the paper. Elaborately pierced and cut borders, simple edgings cut with fancy scissors, long and slender 3-D embellishments, the list is endless and endlessly fascinating.

To make a wide variety of decorative borders, take any basic technique and use repetition to lengthen it. Combining techniques adds extra interest. You might repeat letters to form a border of words, or repeat a cut-out flower the length of a page to form a lacy edge for a wedding card.

The patterns for the paper chain cards shown on pages 28–31 are also perfect to use as borders. You can reduce many of the embellishment patterns and repeat them, turning one simple image into a stunning and slender border treatment.

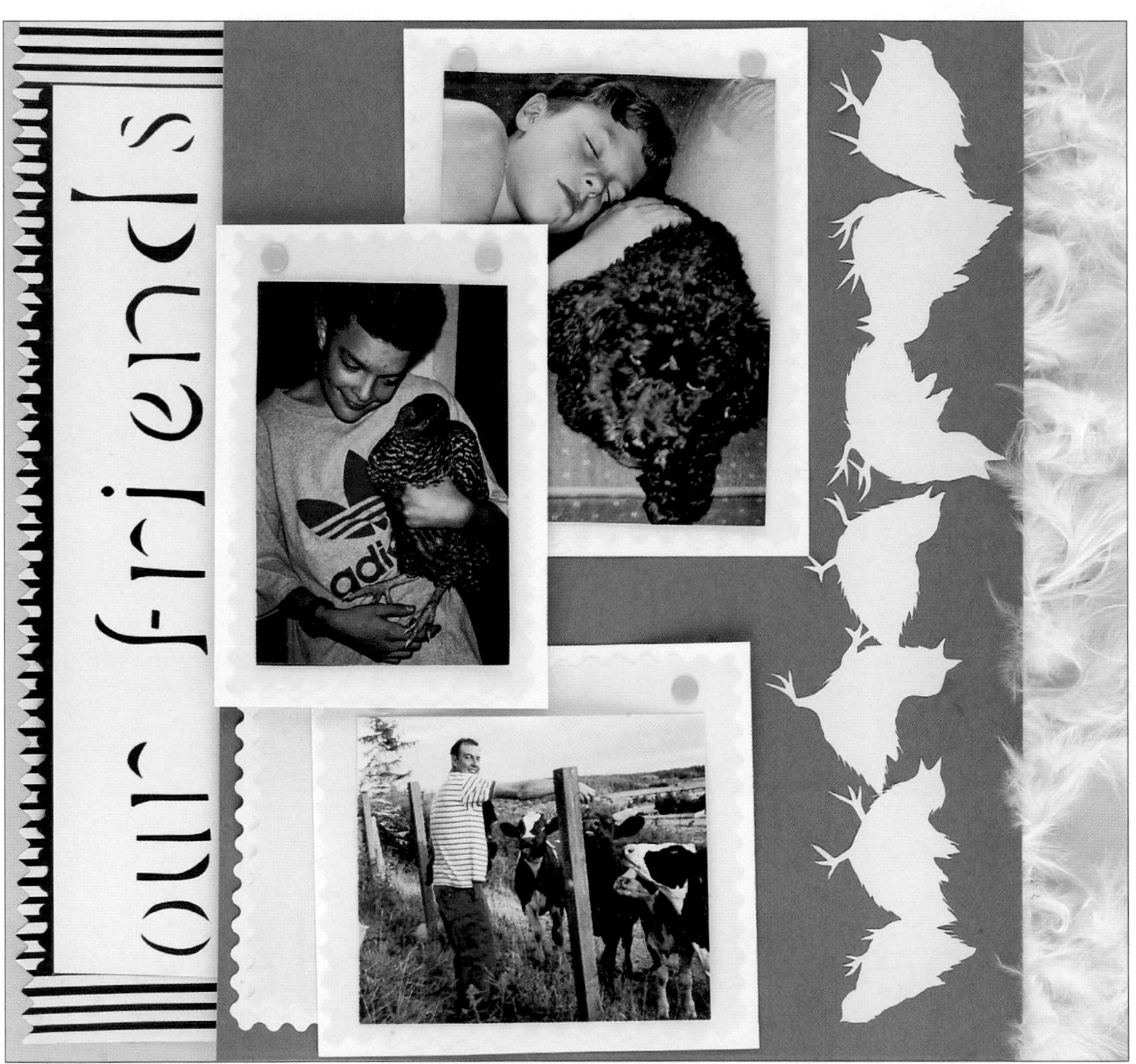

chickens

A squawk of fluffy chicks can decorate almost anything. Use the Lowercase Letters Pattern on page 119 to reproduce the title.

See Chickens Pattern on page 111.

little ducks

This dainty border is just ducky. You can turn it into a frame by cutting out four patterns, assembling into a rectangle, and mitering the corners.

See Little Ducks Pattern on page 103.

Easter Finery
Fancy suspenders & a spiffy green coat. Oh, my!
Aren't we the coolest cousins on the block!

easter parade

Whether you choose clear bright colors, soft pastels, or simple white paper, this pattern makes a fun springtime decoration.

See Easter Parade Pattern on page 111.

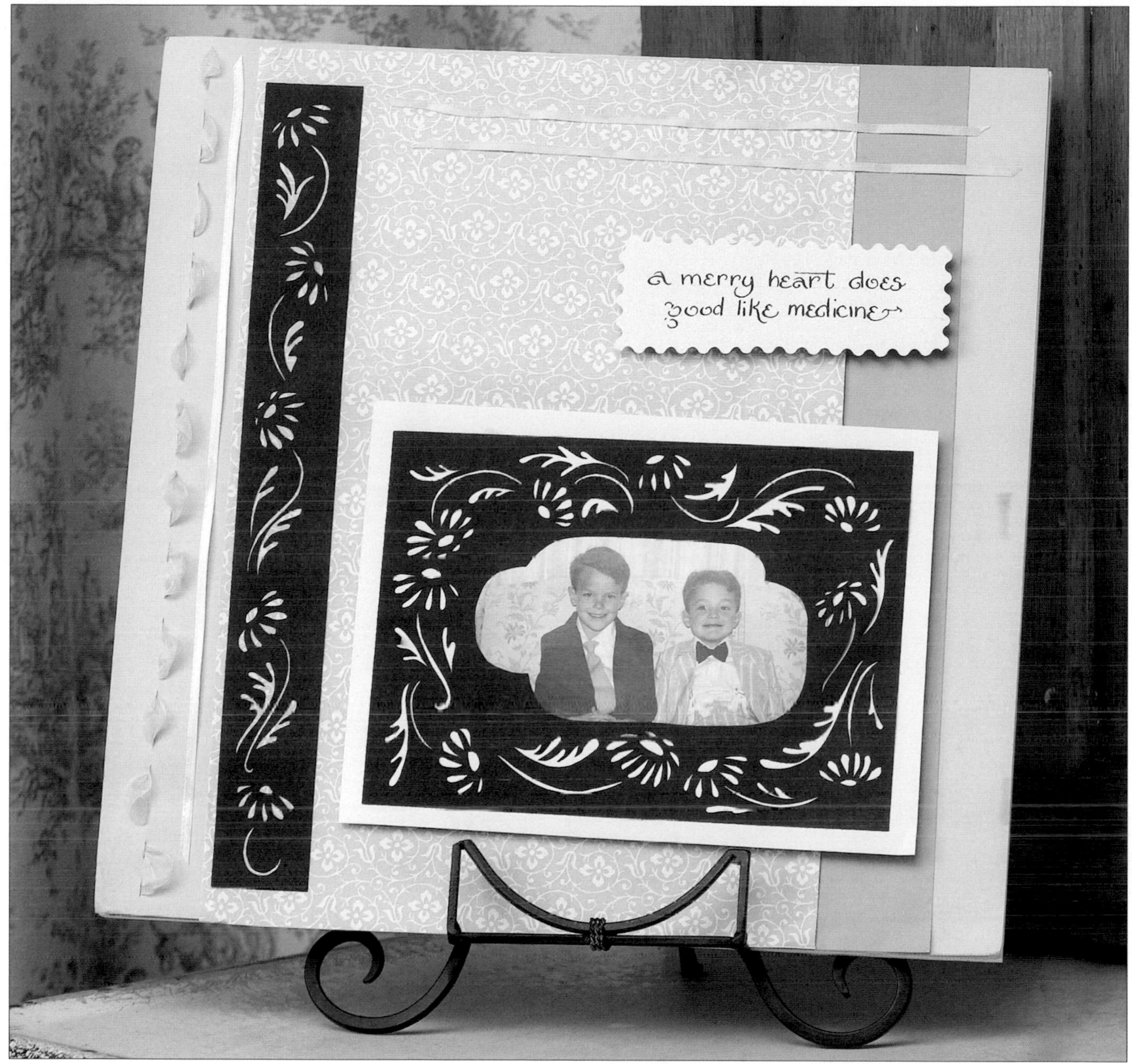

daisy frame & border

This matching set can decorate a scrapbook page, or the frame can be used for a card, with the border glued to the flap of an envelope.

See Daisy Frame & Border Patterns on page 106.

Tips & Tricks

Finding Lightweight Colored Papers

It can be difficult to find solid-color papers that are lightweight enough to cut easily. I use lightweight solid colors that are tough enough not to tear but thin enough to cut smoothly.

wild roses

The irregularities of woody stems make this pattern fun to cut. Try twisting the scissors back and forth as you cut for a not-too-smooth edge. If you're just learning to cut paper, this forgiving design is a good exercise.

See Wild Roses Pattern on page 104.

ferns & briars

Rustic and wild, this leafy piece works well in black as well as shades of green and brown.

See Ferns & Briars Pattern on page 109.

delphinium block & border

You can turn almost any design into a border by elongating or repeating it, or by simply making variations on a theme. In this case, I sat out in the garden and cut out the delphiniums waving in the wind.

See Delphinium Block & Border Patterns on page 110.

Tips & Tricks

Adding Dimension to Borders

Decorative borders need not be flat. You can make them wave up and down with the judicious placement of thick self-adhesive dots or slivers of foam-board.

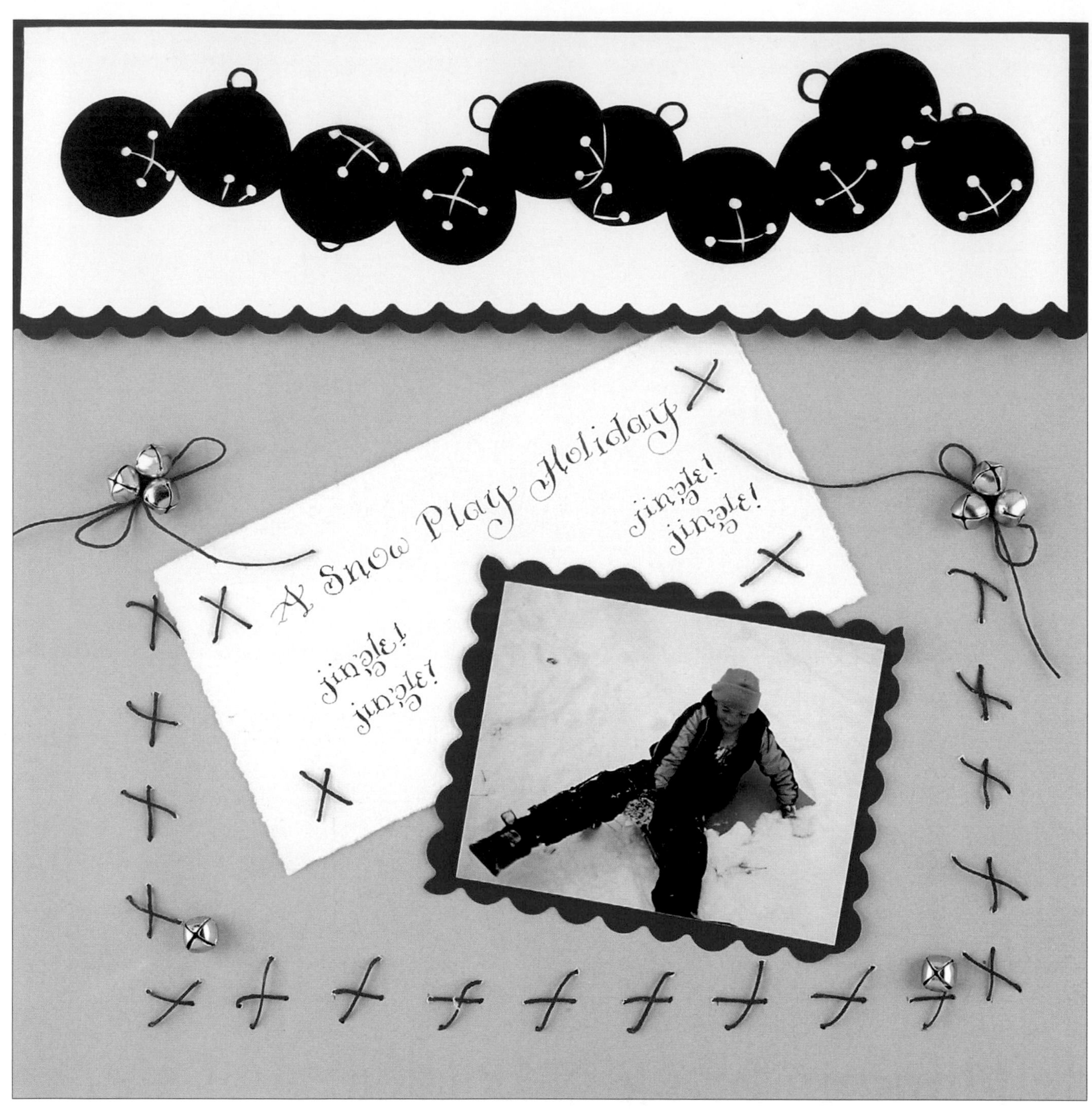

jingle bells

A row of festive jingle bells are a great addition to a winter scrapbook page or holiday card.

See Jingle Bells Pattern on page 117.

holly & berries

Many designs are applicable to a multitude of applications. This one is ideal for scrapbook pages, along the edge of a journal page, or decorating the flap of a special envelope.

See Holly & Berries Pattern on page 111.

We remember Christmases with Nana

santa's holiday parade

O Santa please come quick, and visit these happy boys & girls! The birthday boy is wearing antlers

This merry border also works for cards or a basic ornament if you don't include the trees on the right.

See Santa's Holiday Parade Pattern on page 119.

JOHNSON'S

alphabets

Cut-paper alphabets come in handy for so many projects. A single initial makes a beautifully simple card for any occasion, and I've later found many cards framed and hanging in my friends' homes. Scrapbook pages with hand-cut letters have extra depth, and it's surprisingly fast to cut a few words or a title.

YOU'LL NEED:

- Cardstock
- Glue or glue stick
- Lightweight paper

HERE'S HOW:

1. To use these alphabets straight from the patterns, use a photocopier to size them to fit the project you have in mind. If you will be using multiple letters, one template will suffice.
2. Trace a letter onto the back of the paper, starting at the right-hand side, and move the pattern so that the next letter falls into the correct position.
3. Trace that letter and repeat until finished. Notes: You can do the same thing without a pattern by simply sketching the letters in reverse before you cut. Remember you must start from the right and move to the left. Everything's backward because you're working from the back of the page.
4. Trim cut paper as desired and glue onto a card or scrapbook page.

chunky alphabet

These chunky letters are decidedly informal. I often like to cover them with vintage glitter. See Chunky Alphabet Pattern on page 122.

> *Tips & Tricks*
>
> **Checking Letters Before You Cut**
>
> *A clever way to check that your words will come out properly is to hold the traced pattern up to a mirror. If it looks right in the mirror, you can cut with confidence knowing that the finished product will look like the mirror image.*

letter sign, tag & card

Single letters, cut from lightweight paper with scalloped edges, are mounted on solid-color cardstock, creating a classic monogram motif that is perfect for decorating gift tags and cards. Similarly, you can fashion a simple sign by combining a few letters to make up words.

See Fancy Alphabet Pattern on page 121 and Curlicue Alphabet Pattern on page 120.

(right) fancy alphabet

Arrange letters to create a title for a scrapbook page. Here, the family name is cut from a solid color and paired with two patterned papers and a cherished photo.

See Fancy Alphabet Pattern on page 122.

lowercase letters

These letters are fast and easy to cut and perfectly complement the gentle curves of this floral motif.

See Lowercase Letters Pattern on page 119.

JOHNSON'S

HARPER'S
NEW MONTHLY MAGAZINE.
VOLUME LXXXIV.
DECEMBER, 1891 TO MAY, 1892.
She was known as a rather
flighty child... always
dancing with the fairies
& singing with the birds
Günther
BRUXELLES
RUE NEUVE 25

idea gallery

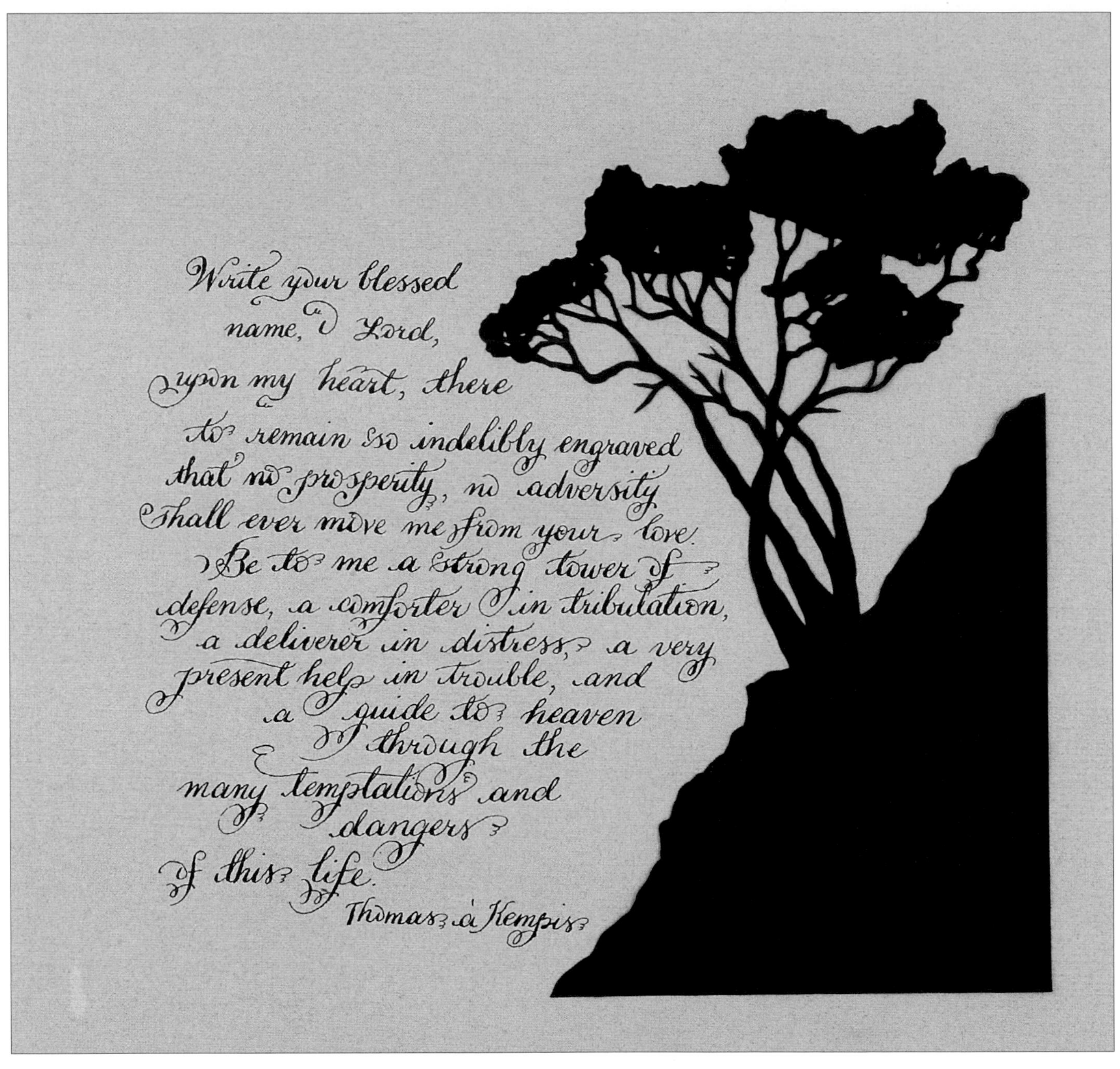

Write your blessed
name, O Lord,
upon my heart, there
to remain so indelibly engraved
that no prosperity, no adversity
shall ever move me from your love.
Be to me a strong tower of
defense, a comforter in tribulation,
a deliverer in distress, a very
present help in trouble, and
a guide to heaven
through the
many temptations and
dangers
of this life.
Thomas à Kempis

My journals are often unconventional, even stark in their simplicity. Sometimes they're pictures without words; sometimes I borrow words from other people. This straightforward piece was made while sailing through the picturesque San Juan Islands off the Washington coast. I used a Thomas à Kempis quote along with a paper-cut of a madrona tree on an island to record the serenity of twilight in the Northwest.

I've learned never to travel without my well-worn little supply box, which contains only the most basic tools: a few sheets of paper, my trusty scissors, a copperplate calligraphy nib in a holder, tiny pots of India ink, and paste. Without my box, I'd have been itching for a way to remember the peaceful moment.

In the rural area where we live, the Fourth of July is still celebrated with parades and picnics. I sat at one of these old-fashioned celebrations and cut out the charming scene. I often forget a camera, but there's always a pair of scissors and some paper in my pocket or purse.

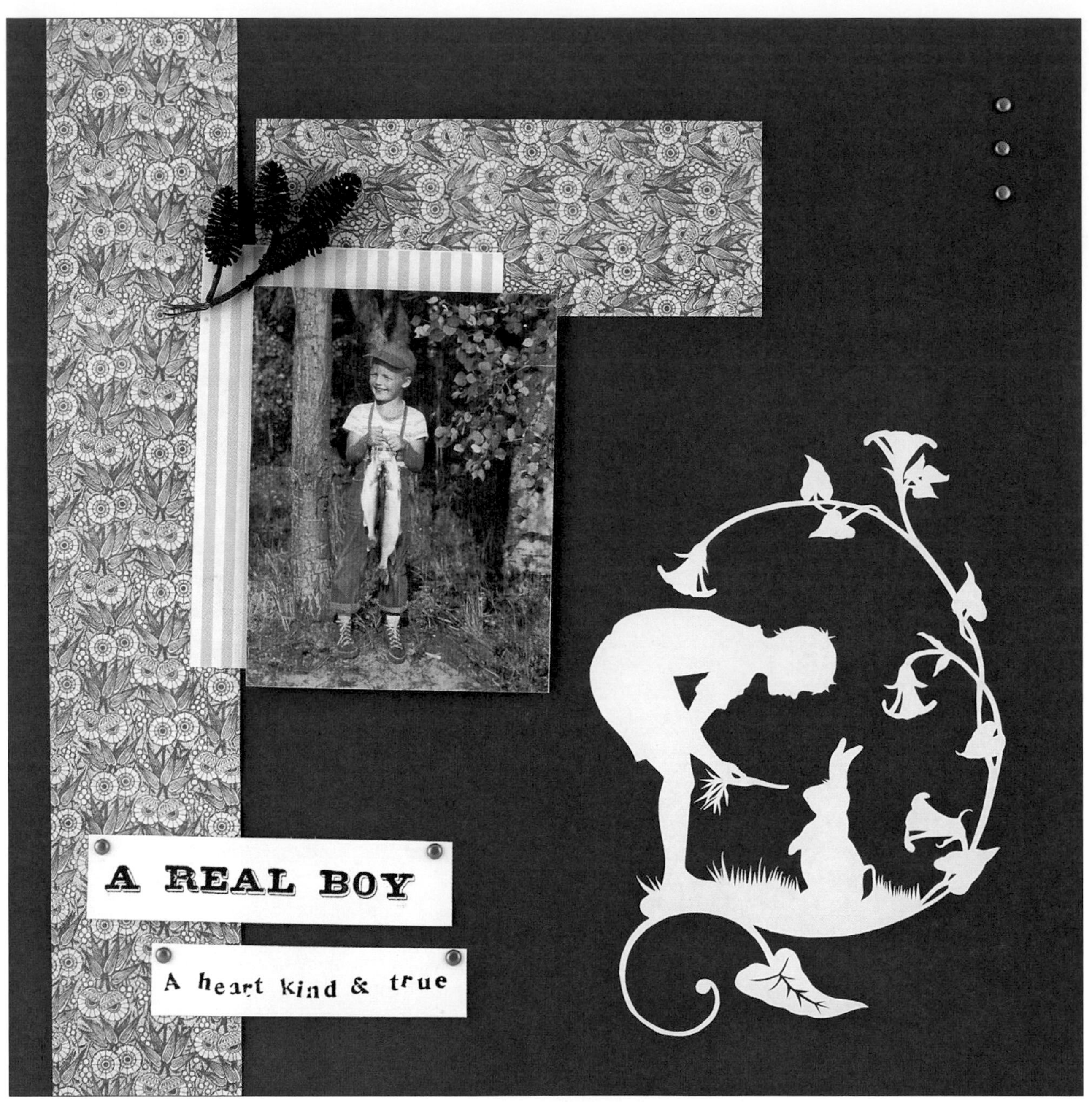
A REAL BOY
A heart kind & true

How do you decide which paper-cut design to pair with which photograph? Sometimes I like to find an element of commonality, such as the boy outdoors shown on this page. Adding captions and 3-D embellishments ties the theme together.

The merriest, jolliest, happiest of holidays always sends me back to my Scandinavian roots. Prancing reindeer are an irresistible theme for me, fresh every year.

I also like to repeat elements in a design. The dots on my merry red paper are echoed in the red berries stitched to a corner with a tiny sprig of pine. People often ask me how I come up with my designs and how they evolve. I am extremely curious by nature, and have always loved to stare at everything around me. I love to sketch with scissors or a pencil. Anything from goats' knees to rosebuds, baby noses to laundry blowing in the wind, captivates my attention.

Fascinated by facial structure and cooking, I did one of my typically messy journals, which led to designs for a series of porcelain tableware. Collections of random quotes and pencil or scissor sketches jammed into a folder sometimes become my favorite and most-used journals.

fairy girl
her eyes twinkle brightly
her lips red as cherries
nose turned up so sweetly
feet swift as fairies'

ARPER'S
NE
THLY MAGAZINE.
OLUME LXXXIV.
DECEMBER, 1891 TO MAY, 1892.
She was known as a rather
flighty child... always
dancing with the fairies
& singing With the birds
Günther
BRUXELLES
RUE NEUVE 25

Whimsical fairies are a favorite theme for me, as are cherubic children. I often use vintage papers or scans of them as background material. For these pages, I also made liberal use of my collection of antique type.

A package of hook-and-eyes in a thrift store called out to me. Paired with old pattern pieces, tags whipped up on a whim, and some embroidery floss cards, it makes for an eye-catching element on a simple yet effective page.

Gingham, lace, and a bit of ribbon set the stage for this tea party scene. This scrapbook page design is perfect for remembering precious moments that celebrate the relationship between mother and daughter.

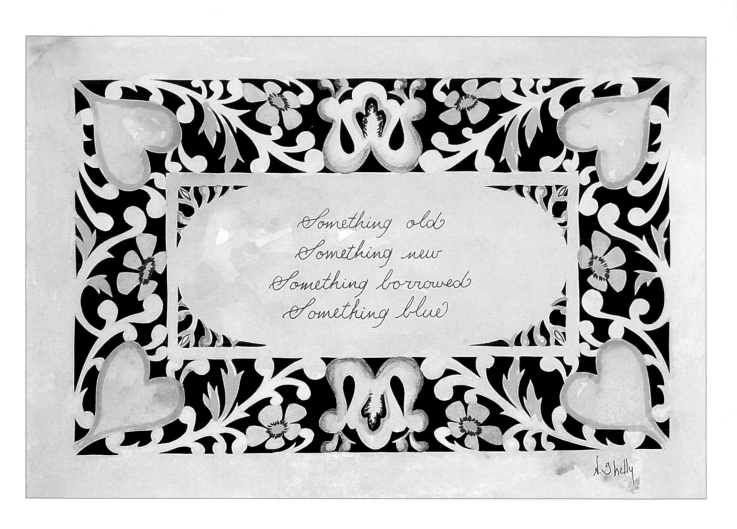

Something old
Something new
Something borrowed
Something blue

N. Shelly

These two cards are the work of Pennsylvania paper cutter Nancy Shelly. The intricate cutting, accomplished with a craft knife, and the use of transparent watercolors are characteristic of Nancy's imaginative work.

Anne Olwin, from Anacortes, Washington, is a prolific watercolor artist, author, and teacher. Her first attempts at cutting paper show an effective blending of the two mediums.

Barbara Trombley is the glitter diva. Her Art Institute Glitters make my heart beat a little bit faster. She not only sells the most wonderful glitters I've ever found but she loves to use it herself. Here are three pieces Barbara made using her sticky paper made especially for capturing the sparkly stuff. Similar to clear contact paper, you can cut a simple design while the backing paper is still on. Then remove the backing and apply glitter.

I like to use dimensional sticky dots instead of glue to adhere it to paper.

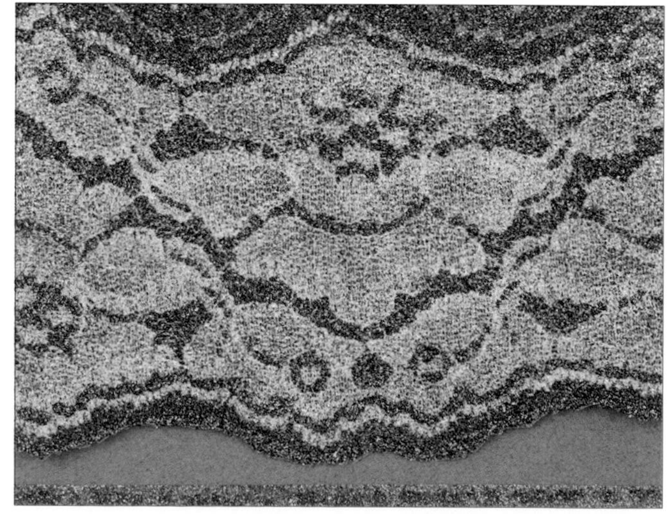

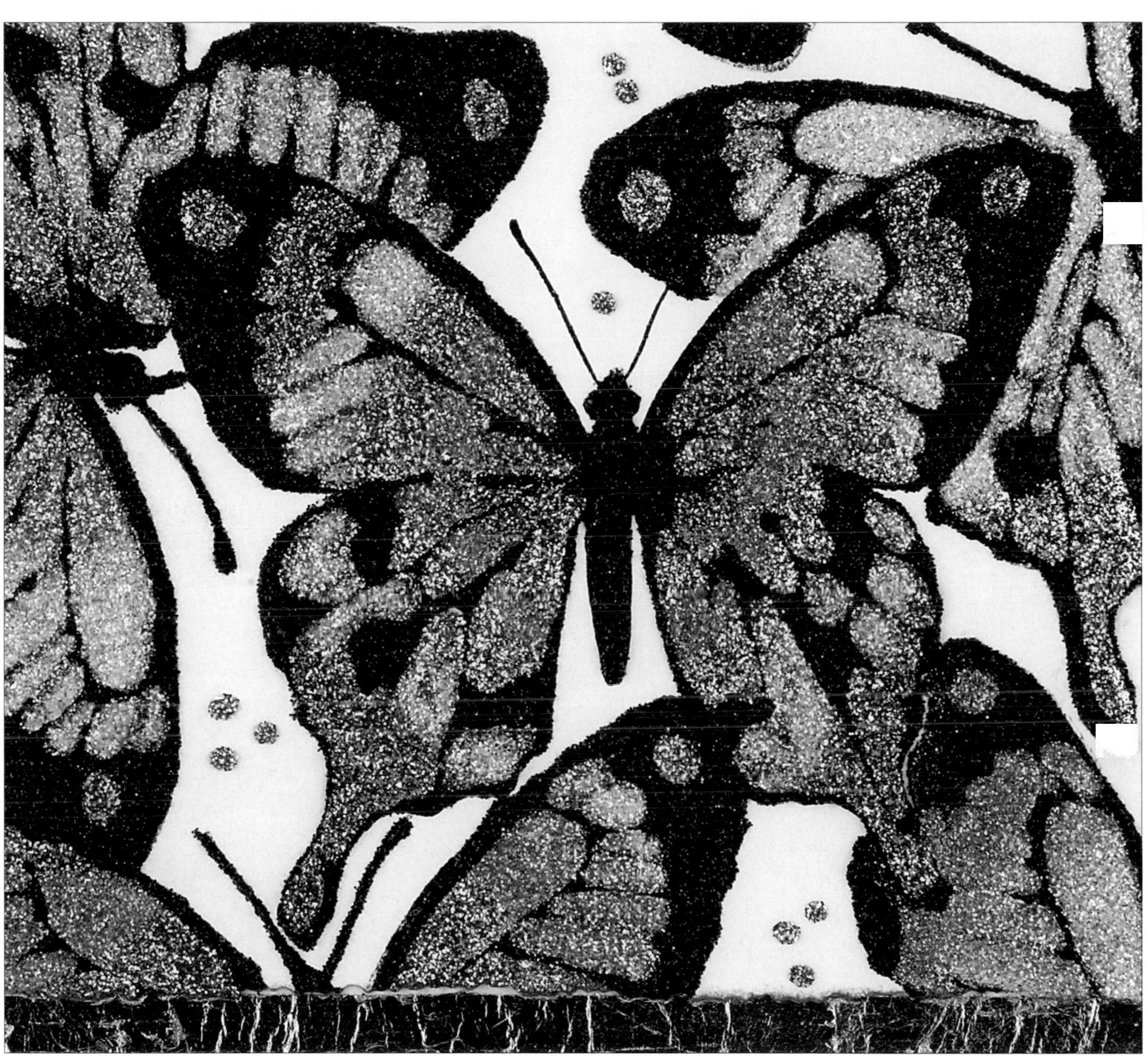

the patterns

LATTICE ROSE PATTERN

It's important to remember that all the patterns in this book are almost endlessly versatile. By changing the size, using only part of a pattern, or repeating a design, you can use these patterns in a million different ways. Let your imagination run; you can use them for a purpose completely different than what's shown in this book.

FROM ONE NUT PATTERN

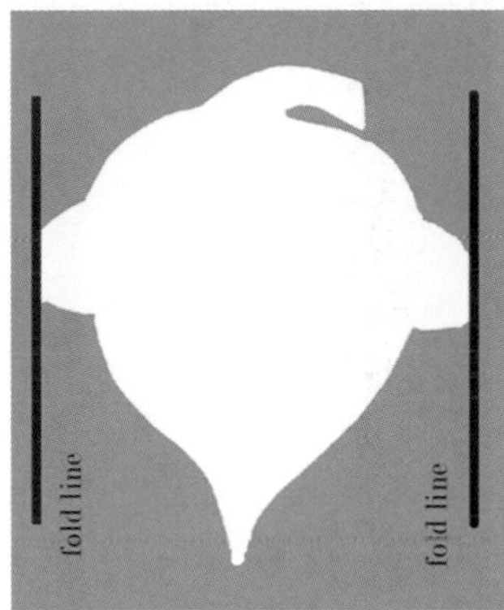

HAND-PAINTED TEACUP PATTERN

FIELD FLOWERS PATTERN

SKIPPING TIME PATTERN

GIRL SKIPPING PATTERN

JOYFUL EASTER PATTERN

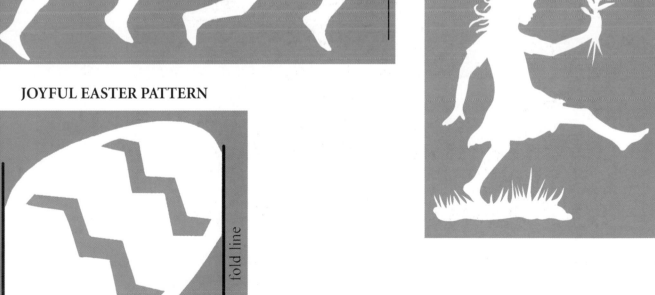

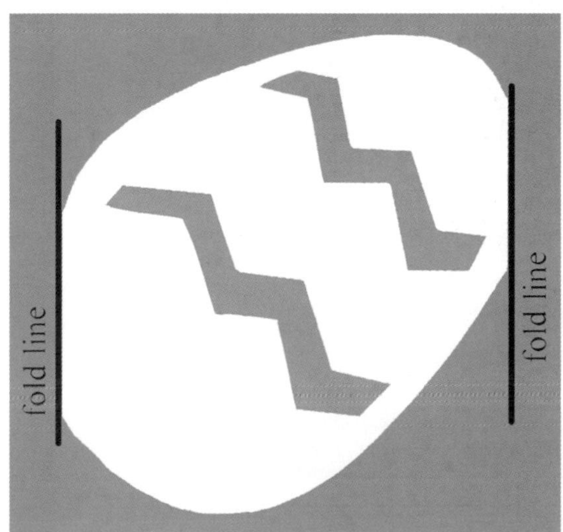

FAIRY GIRLS PATTERN

FLIP-FLOP HEAVEN PATTERN

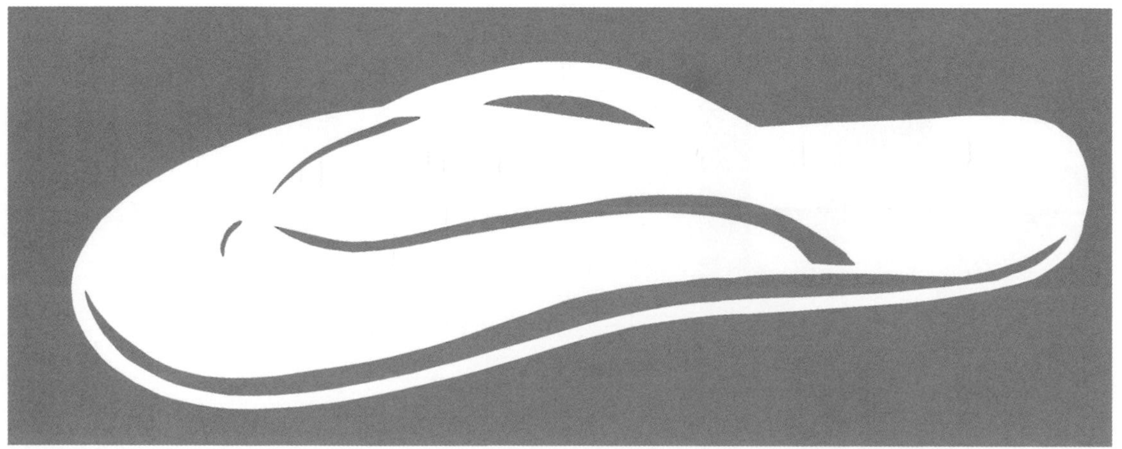

GARDENER'S DELIGHT PATTERN

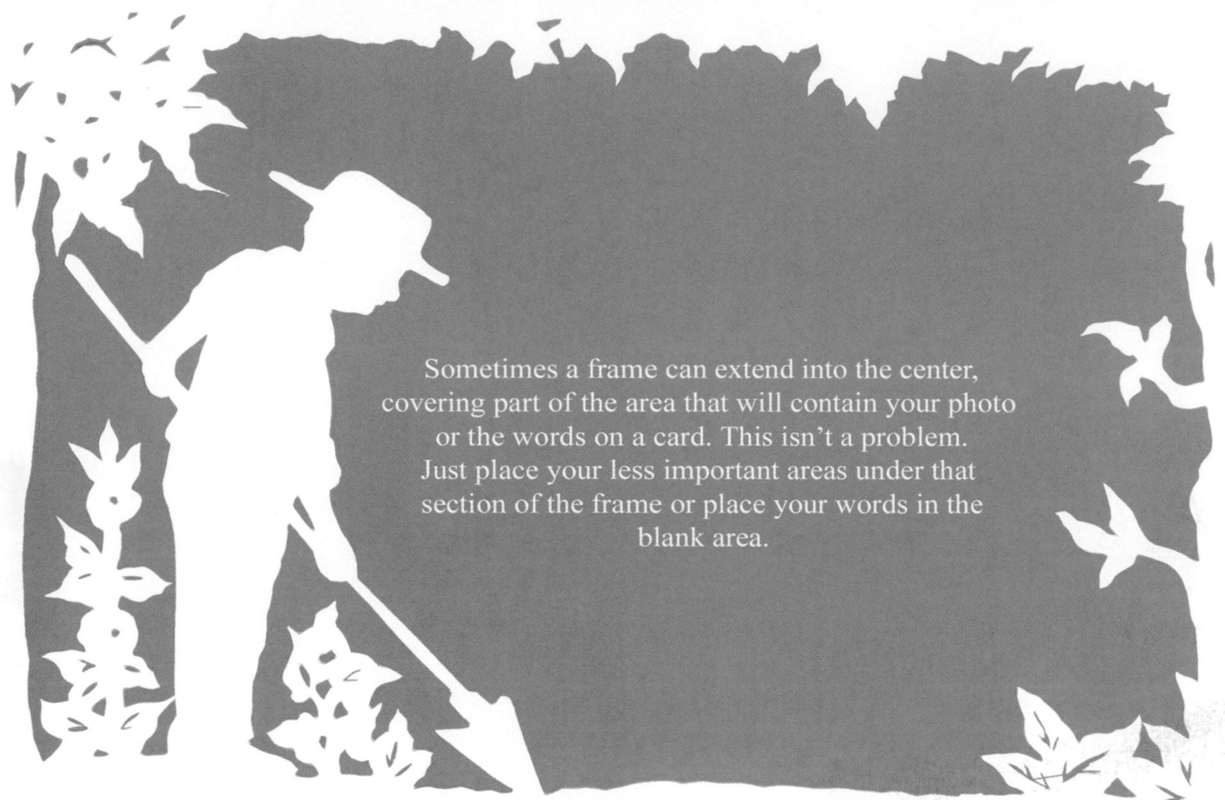

Sometimes a frame can extend into the center,
covering part of the area that will contain your photo
or the words on a card. This isn't a problem.
Just place your less important areas under that
section of the frame or place your words in the
blank area.

SWANS IN A HEART PATTERN

SPRING BOUQUET PATTERN

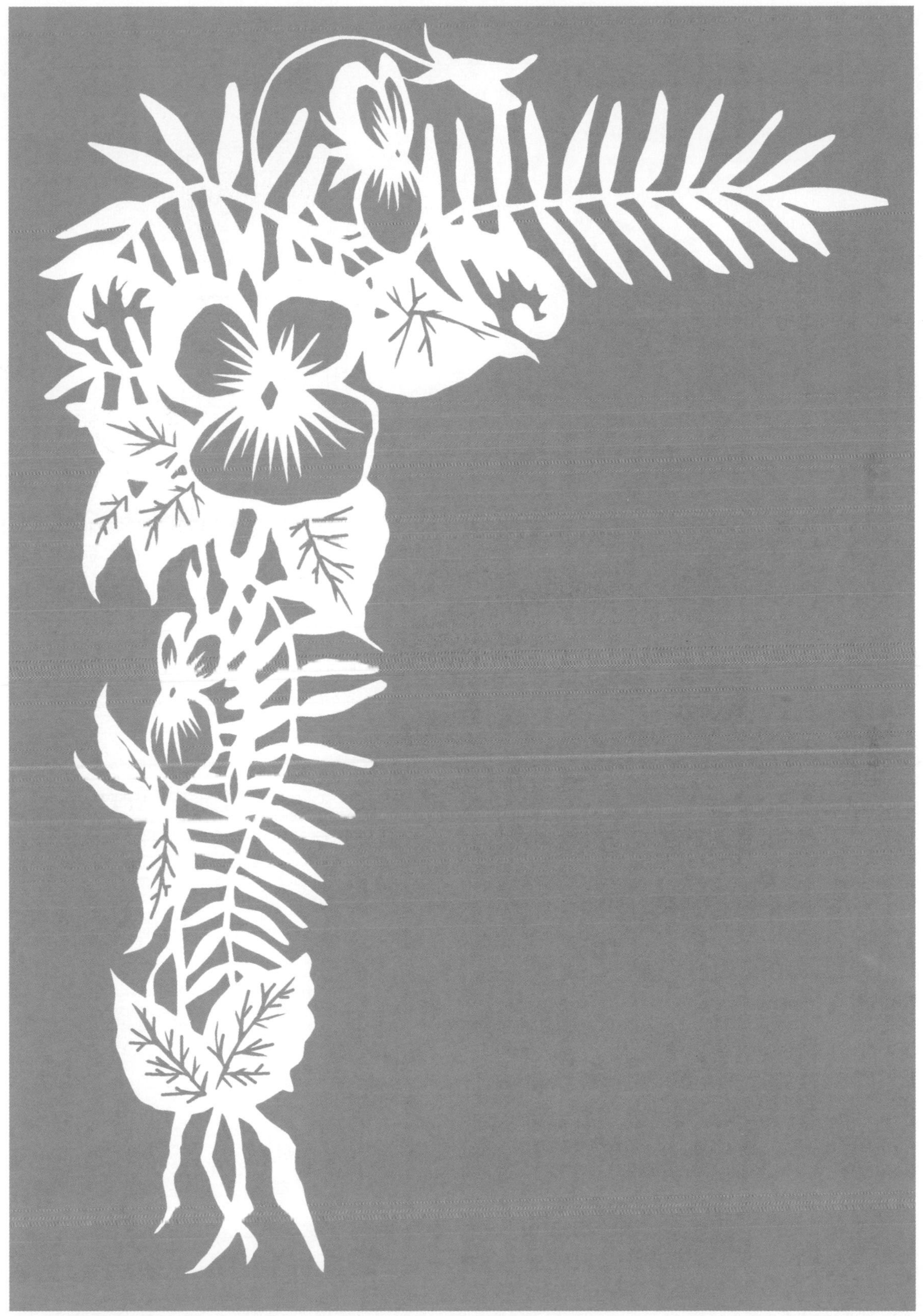

THE FLOWER BASKET PATTERN

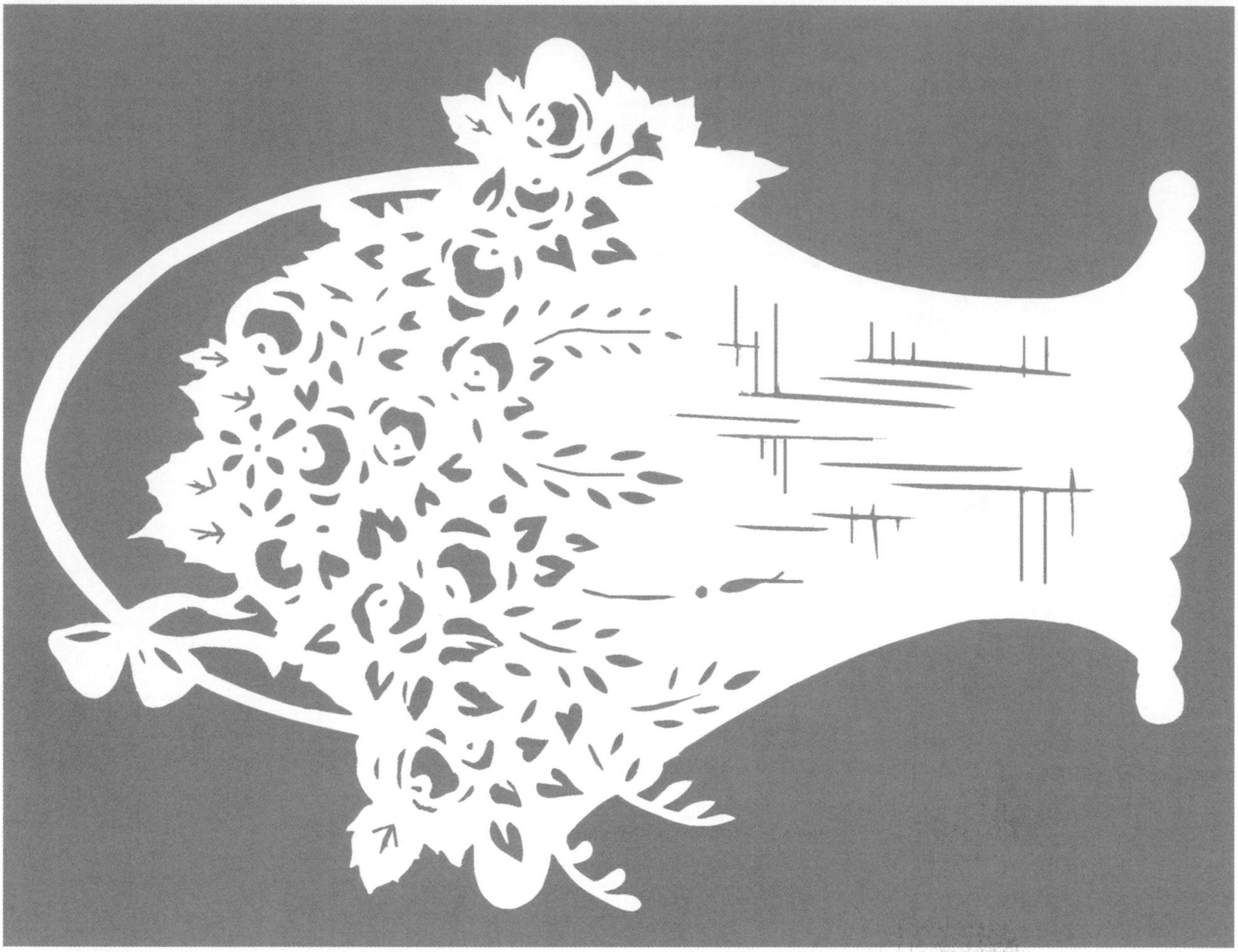

GARDEN FLOWERS PATTERN

ROSE BUSH PATTERN

THE CRADLE PATTERN

LITTLE DUCKS PATTERN

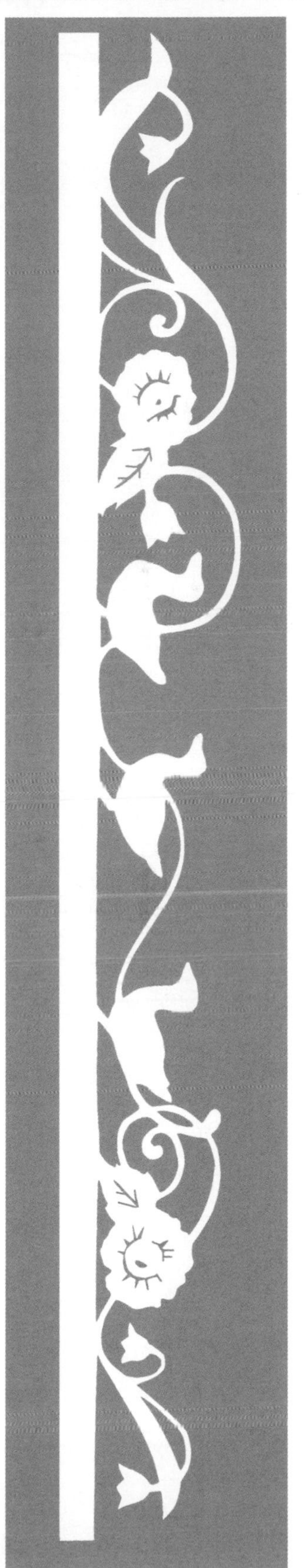

BIRDS ON A TWIG BRANCH PATTERN

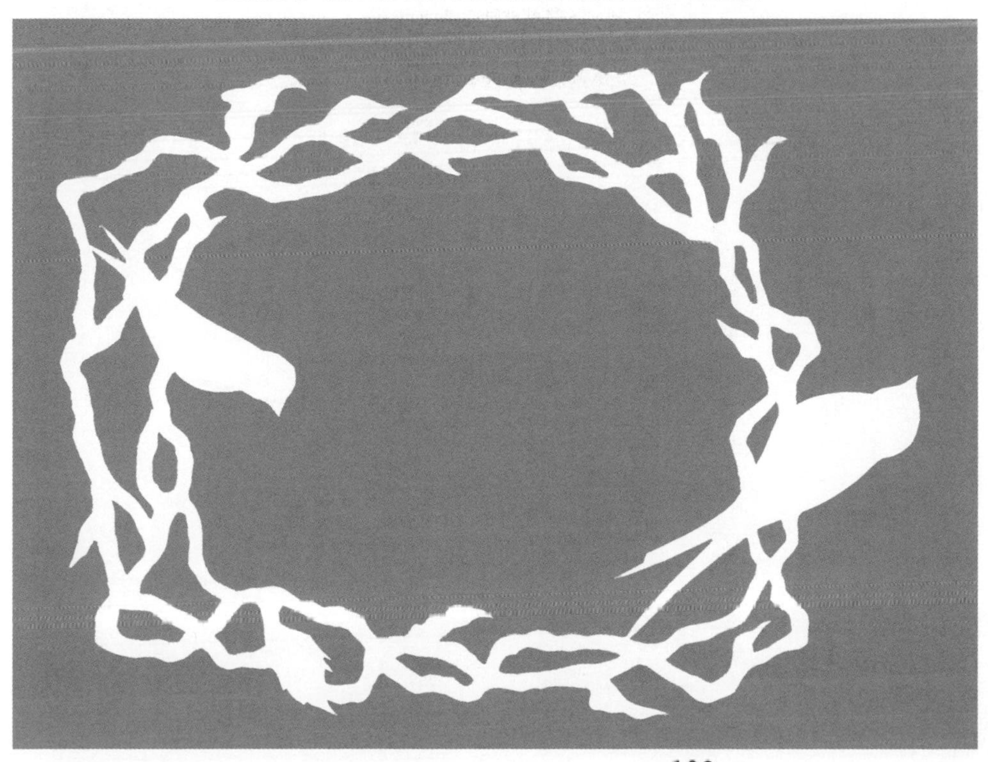

CLIMBING ROSES PATTERN

WILD ROSES PATTERN

FLOWERS & FERNS PATTERN

OUR TOWN PATTERN

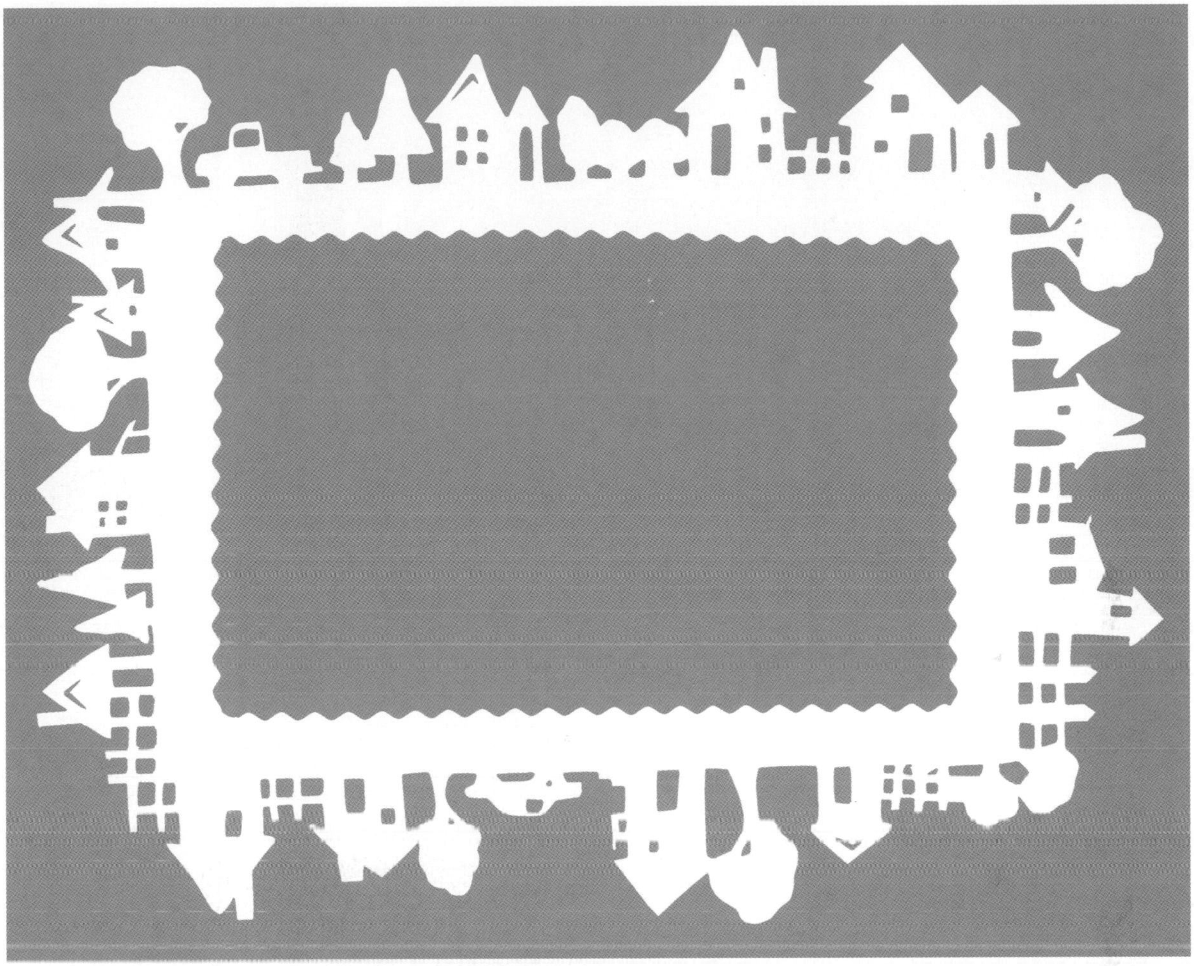

LITTLE HOUSE PATTERN

BEST FRIENDS & BOOKS PATTERN

CUPID PATTERN

STYLISH WOMAN PATTERN

SEA STARS PATTERN

ROSE LEAF PATTERN

ASPEN PATTERN

PEACEFUL BIRDS ON A BRANCH PATTERN

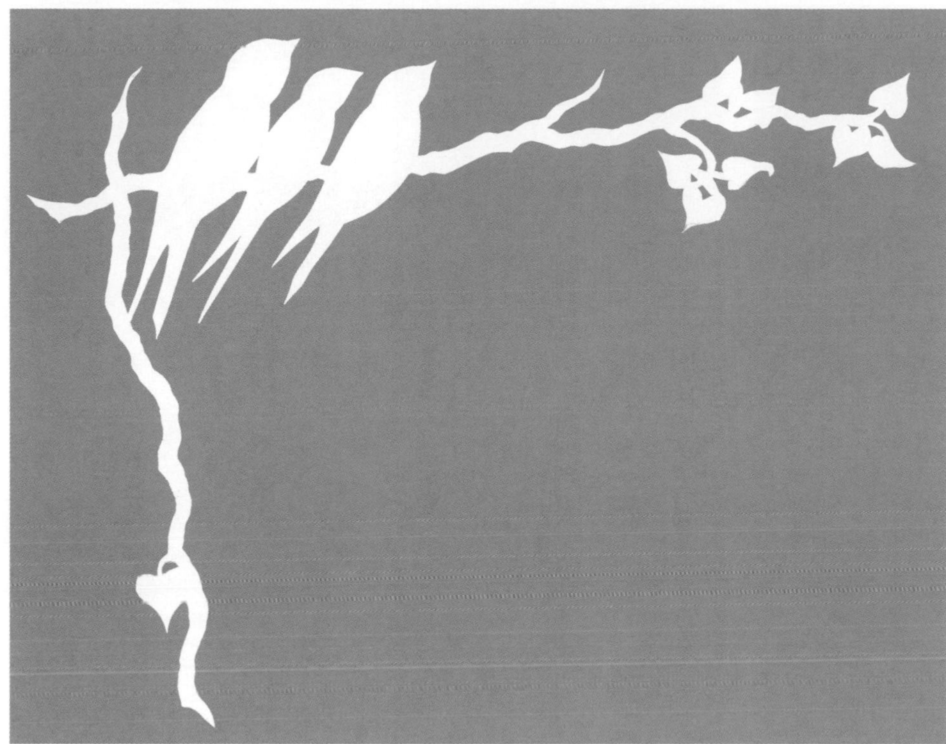

FERNS & BRIARS PATTERN

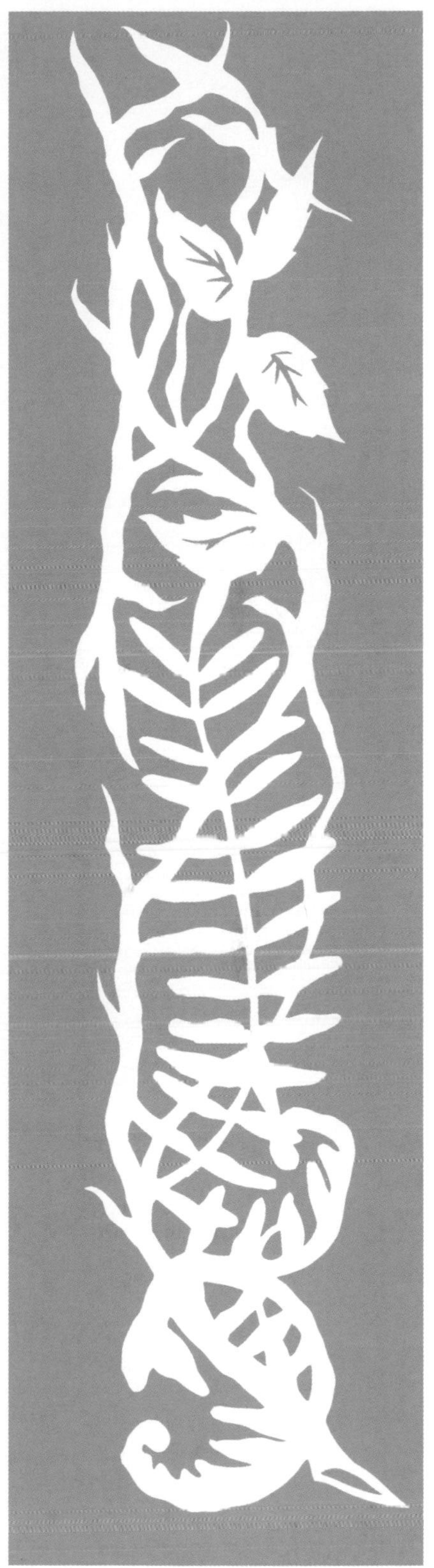

GONE FISHING PATTERN

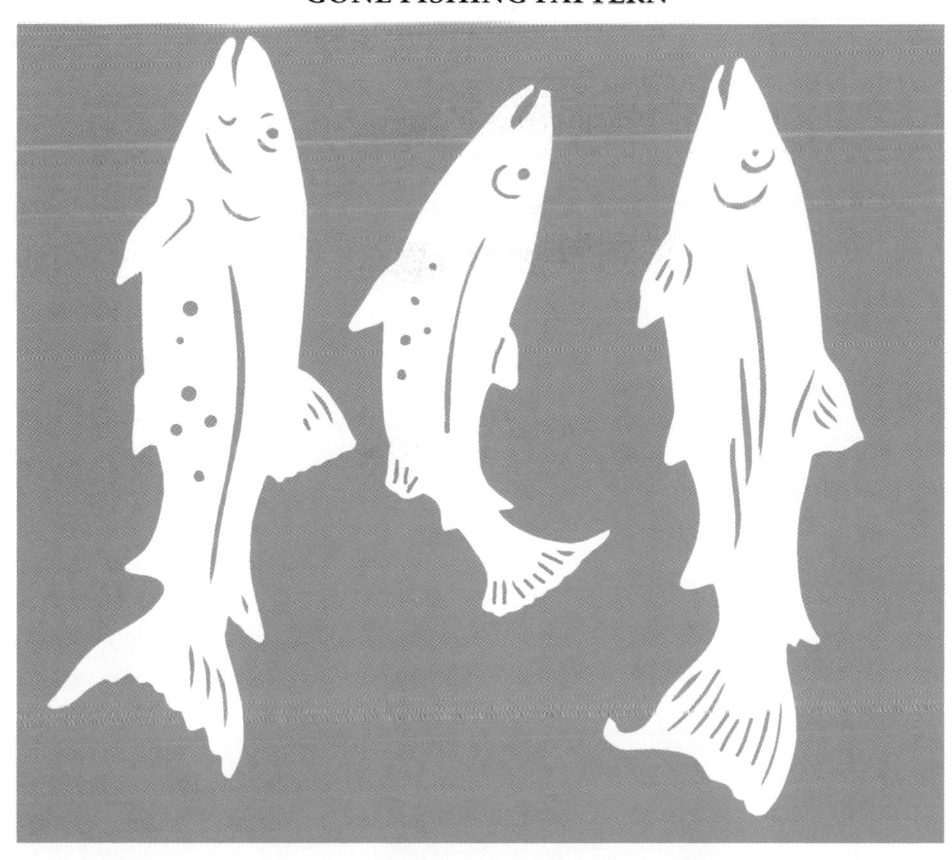

GLOVE PATTERN

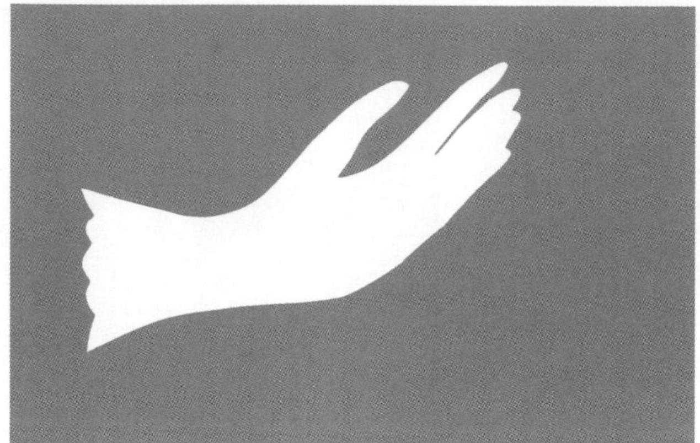

HEELS PATTERNS

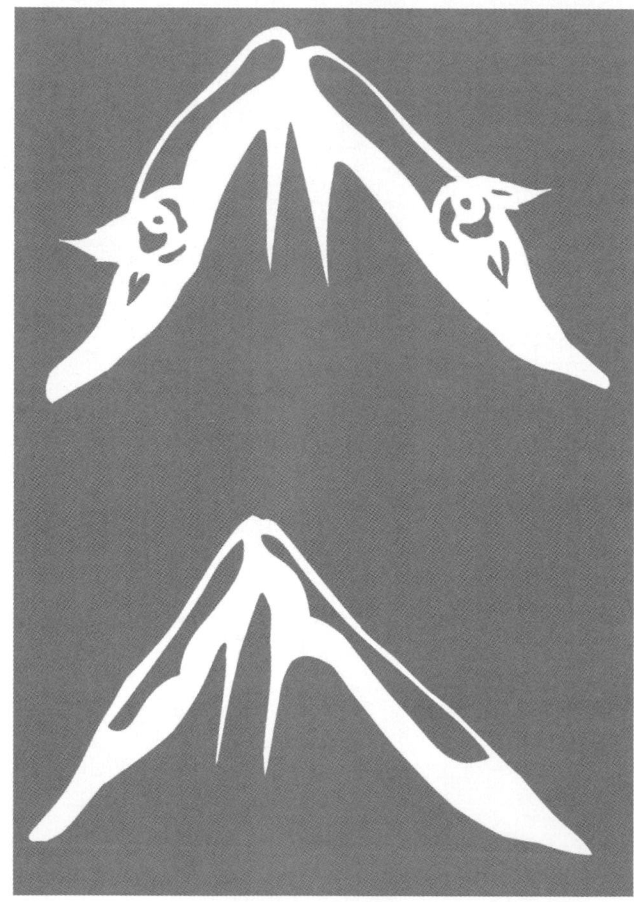

DELPHINIUM BLOCK & BORDER PATTERNS

BLACK DRESS PATTERN

CHICKENS PATTERN

EASTER PARADE PATTERN

HOLLY & BERRIES PATTERN

JOLLY CLOWNS PATTERN

EASTER EGGS PATTERN

BIRDHOUSES & VINES PATTERN

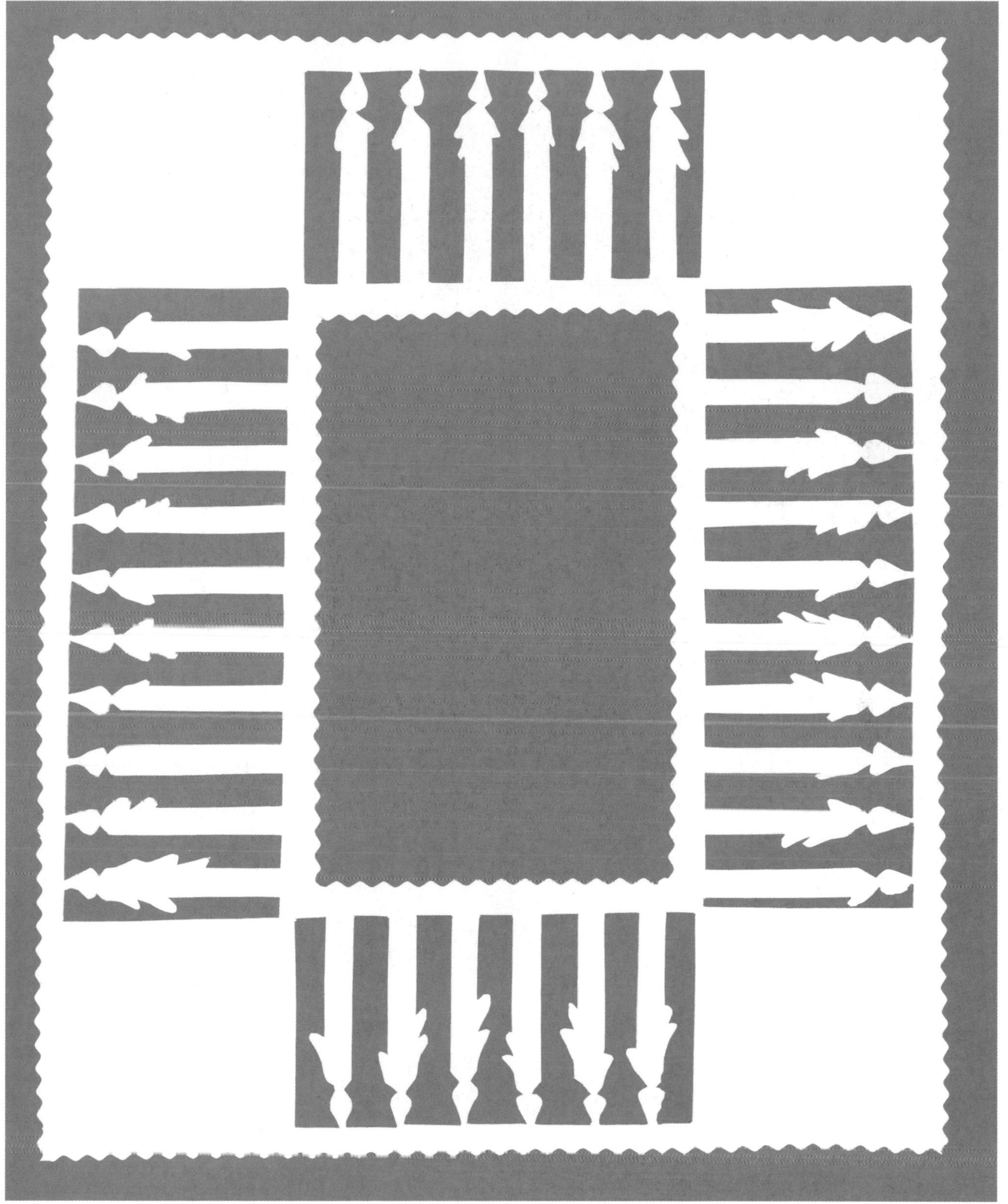

WITCHY HALLOWEEN PATTERN

TRICK OR TREAT PATTERN

JACK-O-LANTERNS PATTERN

SNOW GIRL PATTERN

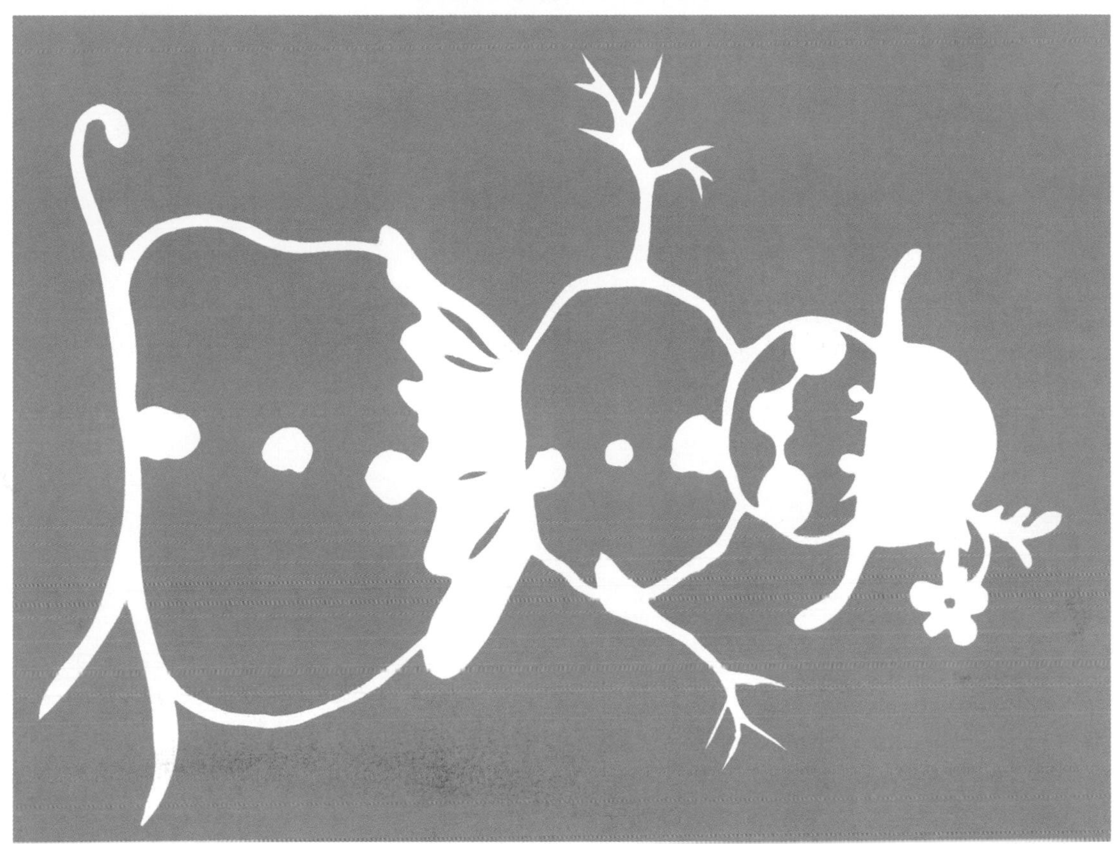

SNOW BOY PATTERN

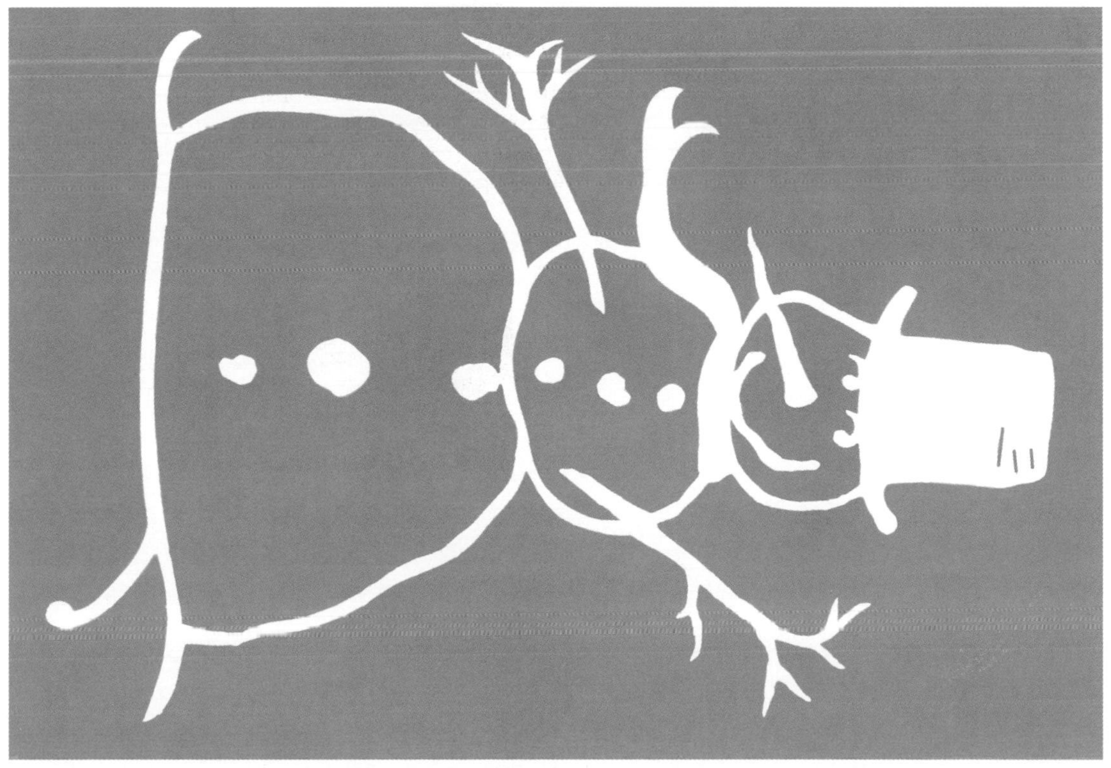

WINTER MITTENS CARD PATTERN

WINTER MITTENS #1 PATTERN

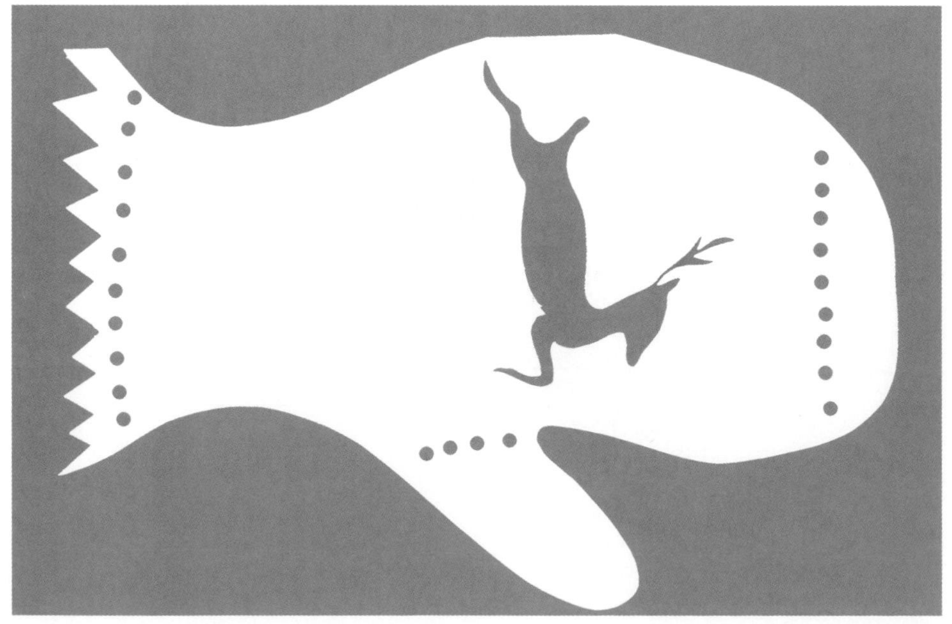

WINTER MITTENS #2 & #3 PATTERNS

JINGLE BELLS PATTERN

SANTA & HIS GIFTS PATTERN

SANTA'S STOCKING PATTERN

SANTA'S HOLIDAY PARADE PATTERN

LOWERCASE LETTERS PATTERN

CURLICUE ALPHABET PATTERN

FANCY ALPHABET PATTERN

CHUNKY ALPHABET PATTERN

CHOCOHOLIC PATTERN

acknowledgments

ART INSTITUTE GLITTER, INC.

Unusual fine glitters and adhesives in a wide variety of colors; sticky paper

712 North Balboa Street

Cottonwood, AZ 86326

Telephone (877) 999-0805

www.artglitter.com

DICK BLICK

Art supplies

P.O. Box 1267

Galesburg, IL 61402-1267

Telephone (800) 828-4548

www.dickblick.com

D. BLUMCHEN & COMPANY

Colorless glitter

P.O. Box 1210

Ridgewood, NJ 07451-1210

Telephone (866) 653-9627

www.blumchen.com

CLEARSNAP

Rollagraph rubber stamps, ink pads, stamping supplies

P.O. Box 98

Anacortes, WA 98221

Telephone (888) 448-4862

www.clearsnap.com

C. R. GIBSON

Manufacturer of albums, stickers, and other supplies, some of which feature Sharyn's artwork

404 BNA Drive, Building 200, Suite 600

Nashville TN 37217

Telephone (800) 243-6004

www.crgibson.com

MAKING MEMORIES

Large selection of hard-to-find lightweight 12" x 12" papers in solid colors

1168 West 500 North

Centerville, UT 84014

Telephone (801) 294-0430

www.makingmemories.com

DANIEL SMITH

Art supplies

P.O. Box 84268

Seattle, WA 98124-5568

Telephone (800) 426-7923

www.danielsmith.com

PLAID ENTERPRISES, INC.

Manufacturer of craft supplies.

Plaid makes All Night Media products, including Sharyn's rubber stamps and cardmaking supplies. Bucilla Needlework is a Plaid brand that produces Sharyn's images in needlepoint and cross-stitch kits.

3225 Westech Drive

Norcross, GA 30092-3500

Telephone (800) 842-4197

www.plaidonline.com

SHARYN SOWELL

Hand-cut paper and product design.

14922 Valley View Drive

Mount Vernon, WA 98273

Telephone (360) 424-5846

www.sharynsowell.com

BOOK PRODUCTION

Editor: Jeanne Bush

Design: Pinnacle Marketing

Photography: Ryne Hazen, Zac Williams, William Wright

Photo Stylist: Rebecca Ittner

about the author

SHARYN SOWELL

Confined to a fishing boat with a pair of restless toddlers and two serious fishermen, Sharyn Sowell used her husband's Swiss army scissors and the children's' lunch bags to cut out Noah and a zoo-full of animals. Merely trying to amuse the boys, Sharyn never suspected she'd just fallen head over heels into a love affair with scissors and paper.

Today, you can find Sharyn hidden away in a tiny rose-covered studio in the corner of her garden, surrounded by scraps and snips of paper, well-loved scissors, old birds' nests, family photographs, and an antique printing press named Alice.

She may be scissoring a pair of fashionable high-heeled shoes, a delicate bouquet of violets, a frieze of merry children, or a plump pastry chef holding his latest creation aloft. Whatever she cuts, Sharyn's designs are full of mirth and imagination.

Sharyn's cut-paper images can be found on a wide variety of products. Tableware, fabric, scrapbooks, journals, stationery, rubber stamps, gifts, wall décor, and more feature her cut paper, watercolor, calligraphy, and digital imagery.

"My work celebrates the miracles we see every day if we open our eyes to the simple pleasures that surround us," says Sharyn, who agrees with Hans Christian Anderson that "real life is the best fairy tale."

metric equivalency chart

mm-millimeters cm-centimeters
inches to millimeters and centimeters

inches	mm	cm	inches	cm	inches	cm
⅛	3	0.3	9	22.9	30	76.2
¼	6	0.6	10	25.4	31	78.7
½	13	1.3	12	30.5	33	83.8
⅝	16	1.6	13	33.0	34	86.4
¾	19	1.9	14	35.6	35	88.9
⅞	22	2.2	15	38.1	36	91.4
1	25	2.5	16	40.6	37	94.0
1¼	32	3.2	17	43.2	38	96.5
1½	38	3.8	18	45.7	39	99.1
1¾	44	4.4	19	48.3	40	101.6
2	51	5.1	20	50.8	41	104.1
2½	64	6.4	21	53.3	42	106.7
3	76	7.6	22	55.9	43	109.2
3½	89	8.9	23	58.4	44	111.8
4	102	10.2	24	61.0	45	114.3
4½	114	11.4	25	63.5	46	116.8
5	127	12.7	26	66.0	47	119.4
6	152	15.2	27	68.6	48	121.9
7	178	17.8	28	71.1	49	124.5
8	203	20.3	29	73.7	50	127.0

yards to meters

yards	meters	yards	meters	yards	meters	yards	meters	yards	meters
⅛	0.11	2⅛	1.94	4⅛	3.77	6⅛	5.60	8⅛	7.43
¼	0.23	2¼	2.06	4¼	3.89	6¼	5.72	8¼	7.54
⅜	0.34	2⅜	2.17	4⅜	4.00	6⅜	5.83	8⅜	7.66
½	0.46	2½	2.29	4½	4.11	6½	5.94	8½	7.77
⅝	0.57	2⅝	2.40	4⅝	4.23	6⅝	6.06	8⅝	7.89
¾	0.69	2¾	2.51	4¾	4.34	6¾	6.17	8¾	8.00
⅞	0.80	2⅞	2.63	4⅞	4.46	6⅞	6.29	8⅞	8.12
1	0.91	3	2.74	5	4.57	7	6.40	9	8.23
1⅛	1.03	3⅛	2.86	5⅛	4.69	7⅛	6.52	9⅛	8.34
1¼	1.14	3¼	2.97	5¼	4.80	7¼	6.63	9¼	8.46
1⅜	1.26	3⅜	3.09	5⅜	4.91	7⅜	6.74	9⅜	8.57
1½	1.37	3½	3.20	5½	5.03	7½	6.86	9½	8.69
1⅝	1.49	3⅝	3.31	5⅝	5.14	7⅝	6.97	9⅝	8.80
1¾	1.60	3¾	3.43	5¾	5.26	7¾	7.09	9¾	8.92
1⅞	1.71	3⅞	3.54	5⅞	5.37	7⅞	7.20	9⅞	9.03
2	1.83	4	3.66	6	5.49	8	7.32	10	9.14

index

The End